TODAY'S CHILDREN
AND YESTERDAY'S HERITAGE

TODAY'S CHILDREN
and Yesterday's Heritage

A Philosophy of Creative Religious Development

by

Sophia Lyon Fahs

with an introduction by
Angus H. MacLean

THE BEACON PRESS · BOSTON

Contents

Contents

Preface

IN THIS ATTEMPT to set forth an emerging philosophy of religious education, we have dwelt especially on those points where the natural approach to religious development stands in marked contrast to the traditional approach of authority and indoctrination. As a result, the differences between the two ways have been made more clear-cut than they usually appear in practice. These contrasts have been emphasized purposely because we believe that there are profound philosophical differences between these two ways. The changes going on that are significant are not mere changes in methods and techniques of teaching: they cut deep into the religious beliefs and emotions of our time.

Such a philosophy as has been described here is still young. We do not have the support of centuries of wisdom and art behind us. We are searching for new words and new thoughts. Indeed, we stand aquiver on the threshold of a new day; none sees clearly what is in the distance beyond our present experience. The possibilities are as yet untried. But there is a thrill and a glowing hope in being part of a young movement, even though it be small and may long be unpopular.

We are convinced that the religions of mankind will continue to change as every living thing must do. We believe our children should be made aware of the reality and the possibilities in these changes. We believe it is important from what beliefs we mold our action. We believe it is even more important how we determine our beliefs and with what sincerity we keep them.

The difference between the traditional ways of religious guidance and the natural ways has to be tasted to be appreciated. One cannot point the finger and say: "Lo, it is here!" or, "Lo, there it lies!" — for the distinctive flavor permeates the entire relationship between teacher and child, and between all of us and the Unknown. This book is an invitation to those who have not yet dared to adventure wholeheartedly along the natural ways of spiritual guidance to do so, and thus to learn for themselves wherein their values lie.

SOPHIA LYON FAHS

Introduction

To SOME THIS BOOK WILL BE the saying of things they have
dimly sensed and experienced but never brought fully to the
point of articulation. To some it will be a surprising and
happy opening of new doors to understanding and action. To
some it will be a buzz bomb. If this book does not make its
weight felt upon our thinking and practicing in the field of
religious education, the fault will be ours and not the author's.

What we believe is important. When we read what Mrs.
Fahs says about the consequences of some things children are
made to believe, we shall have no doubt about that. How we
acquire our beliefs is, perhaps, even more important, for the
way we get hold of and deal with beliefs must be grounded in
reality if our teaching and learning are to be consistent with
the process of harmonious and happy maturing. Doors must
be left open to new truth. Minds must be equipped to deal
with new and unpredictable problems. Spirits must not be
chained by fear or smothered in guilt.

Mrs. Fahs has sifted the findings of modern child study and
explored the religious strivings of primitive man in her search
for what and how to teach. What comes out of this search
is compelling in its impact and, in places, startling in its implications. Familiar concepts such as respect for persons,
love and democracy appear in this book with a freshness of
insight that makes them new. Let no one be certain that he
loves his child as intelligently as he ought until he reads this
book. Psychological concepts hit us from its pages with new
power. When we see, for example, the stage-by-stage development of a child's emotions, the relation of his growing sense
of values to maturity, and of his ethical concepts and behavior, we cannot escape the challenge to our moralistic

judging and correcting of children. "Judge not, that ye be not judged" — what new power in that old warning! I do not see how any moderately intelligent teacher can read this book without feeling the necessity of making radical changes in curriculum and method, and in his or her own ideas of what is good for — and in — children.

After analyzing the natural curiosities of children against the background of what is known about human nature and the universe and of human culture, the author turns to the choices we have to make, and vividly sketches pictures of the old and the new from which we have to make our choices. The Old Bible with its plan of salvation in contrast to the newly interpreted Bible; the old cosmologies against the new cosmological explorations of our time that have literally created a new heaven and a new earth for us; the old brotherhood that was contingent upon the acceptance of the "one and only way" to salvation, and which divided mankind into the good and the bad, the redeemed and the damned, not only on this earth but for all eternity, and placed man eternally in a state of war — all this against a new and an unqualified brotherhood. Although we liberals have dropped many of the old ideas, we have clung pretty much to the old general pattern. This book gives us not only new wine, but new wineskins. The old concept of the Kingdom of God, for example — how we have clung to the old words! When we read what this volume has to say about it, we know that we really believe in something quite different.

Perhaps the point of most powerful impact is where the author shows some of the implications of the findings of psychiatry for our moralizing habits, and even for our ethical concepts. We liberals have generally felt that we were pretty sound in our ethical thinking. When we read this book, we may change our opinion of ourselves. We tend still to attack evil in dualistic terms, to "fight" it, to "go to war" against it, to think of good and evil in terms of black and white. This part of the book is sure to stir the thinking of all thoughtful people. It *may* stir up controversy. When books describing the so-called "permissive" relationship between counselor and client, or between play director and child, are read along with this book, we can scarcely fail to realize that we are well along in the process of changing our basic thinking about good and evil as well as about personality development and nurture. What this fact promises in modification of our educational and our worshiping practices, and of our relations with peoples and persons generally, can hardly be guessed at present. We only know that changes are impending which may outdo in significance much that has happened to us culturally in the last thousand years.

This is a book about heaven and earth, about history, about various sciences, about religions and cultures, about teachers and parents and children. What is gleaned in new wisdom from all these areas is brought challengingly to bear on both the historic and the prevailing notions of spiritual nurture. It is a book of stirring insights for educational workers, indeed for all who work with people. It is a profound philosophical book. In my opinion, all the philosophers who ever produced anything of lasting worth were those who were personally involved in serving their fellow men. Mrs. Fahs is such a one. She is primarily and always a teacher of children, a very thoughtful one, a teacher whose love for children has driven her to raise fresh questions about the mystery of our beings and of the universe. That is why she has been compelled to become a philosopher. When someone loves thoughtfully and courageously enough to challenge anything, listen to him!

ANGUS H. MACLEAN

Dean, The Theological School
St. Lawrence University

Acknowledgments

A NUMBER OF YEARS of experience in teaching and in directing church schools are in the background of this book. To name all those to whom I am indebted for awakening or for correcting my thinking would be to name all the teachers with whom I have worked, all the children from whom I have learned, and all the books I have read. To list these is clearly impossible. Such is life — a continual receiving and giving until none can know the original sources of his own special gifts.

The Committee on Curriculum and Worship of the Division of Education of the American Unitarian Association is responsible for urging me to write the substance of this philosophy, and they generously relieved me of certain editorial responsibilities in order to make it possible for me to do so. For fifteen years, the Rev. Ernest W. Kuebler — the director of the Division of Education — and this committee and I have been working together to build a library of books for children and teachers of children, in which this philosophy is being implemented. Called the Beacon Series in Religious Education, it is published by the Beacon Press. Although I am assured that all of the committee are in sympathy with this general point of view, it is important to point out that I have not spoken for them — even though they seem pleased that I have spoken.

In writing Chapter 8, "Old and New Cosmologies," I felt a special need to have the accuracy of the statements examined by men of recognized authority with a scientific and philosophic background. It was most fortunate, therefore, that Dr. O. P. Reiser, professor of philosophy at the University of Pittsburgh, and Dr. Daniel Alpert and Dr. Bernard Lewis, both noted physical scientists, read the chapter and gave me their criticisms. I am confident that the chapter has been considerably improved as a result of their comments, which I endeavored to follow with care; but it must be understood that they are not responsible for any infelicities that may still remain in my presentation.

I have profited much by the criticisms given by certain other friends who have read portions of the book: Dr. Floyd Ross, of the University of Southern California; Rev. Irving R. Murray, minister of the First Unitarian Church of Pittsburgh; my son, Dr. Charles B. Fahs; my daughter, Dr. Dorothy Fahs Beck; and the members of the Committee on Curriculum and Worship with whom I have worked. Two other good friends carefully read the entire manuscript, Mrs. Edith F. Hunter and Miss Constance Young. The insights and criticisms rendered me by all of these collaborators have caused many a revision in my presentation, which has affected not only the language, but the thought as well.

S. L. F.

TODAY'S CHILDREN
AND YESTERDAY'S HERITAGE

1

It Matters What We Believe

Science without religion is lame, religion without science
is blind.

— ALBERT EINSTEIN

A SUPERFICIAL REVIEW of modern life often gives the impression that religion is an unimportant concern. It is casually remarked that what one believes matters little; all that is important is how one lives. The history of civilization, however, is one long witness to the power of religious beliefs in affecting mankind's behavior. The noblest as well as the most ruthless of men have been motivated by what they believed about God. Rightly or wrongly, humanity in general has regarded its religious beliefs as having high significance.

Because of religious beliefs men have gone to war. They have sacrificed physical comforts, health and home in order to promulgate their faith in foreign lands among those whose beliefs were different from their own. Because of religious beliefs men have been persecuted, imprisoned, burned and crucified. When the religious beliefs of a nation have been destroyed or radically revised, the course of history has been changed. Our own nation was born because our forefathers could not endure the forcible repression of what they believed. Religious beliefs permeate the world's literature, art and music. No one can understand the history of any people at any period who does not understand its religion.

Religious beliefs have gathered such importance that most people now equate *being religious* with *believing*. Religious

3

people are the "believers" and the unreligious are the "unbelievers." Indeed, loyalty to a set of beliefs has been made the condition of membership in most religious societies — at least in the Western world. Almost every one of the varied Protestant denominations began its separate existence because certain beliefs were either newly affirmed or boldly denied. Belief in these newly organized doctrines then became the basis for membership in these religious bodies. Some formal statement of belief has been and still is the pledge by which admission into most Christian churches is gained. Repetition of the creed Sunday by Sunday has become the usual ritual that signifies acceptability within the fold. Even the newly organized World Council of Churches grants membership only to those willing to sign a statement of their belief in Jesus Christ as Lord and Savior of the world. Indeed, such affirmations of belief are commonly regarded among Christians as the "shibboleth," or the mark on the forehead, by which the guardian of heaven will know for whom to open the gates to a happy eternity. Rightly or wrongly, the world generally has regarded its religious beliefs as matters of supreme importance.

The recent revival of concern for religion has been due in large measure to this conviction regarding the importance of religious beliefs in our society. Belief in God and eternity, in his moral law or in his divine Savior, are thought to be a necessary bulwark against immorality and crime.

Furthermore, our religious beliefs have become the sacred symbols of our personal emotional security. They have stilled our fears and fed our hopes. They are bound up with our most poignant memories, our moments of greatest fearfulness or of greatest ecstasy. Our beliefs have given us the courage we have needed to face tragedy and death. So deeply important can one's religious beliefs become that any condition or event that threatens one's power to hold on to his faith spells emotional catastrophe.

Modern psychoanalysts have admitted, perhaps sometimes begrudgingly, the important role of religious beliefs in the making of personality. "Among my patients in the second half of life — that is to say, over thirty-five," wrote Dr. C. G. Jung, "there has not been one whose problem in the last resort was not that of finding a religious outlook on life. It is safe to say that every one of them fell ill because he had lost that which the living religions of every age have given to their followers, and none of them has been really healed who did not regain his religious outlook."[1]

Although not all psychoanalysts would agree with Dr. Jung at this point, nevertheless an increasing number among them have discovered the dangers involved, and even the possible devastation of personality that may occur, when sincerely held religious beliefs are seriously disturbed. In fact, psychoanalysts generally have become so keenly aware of the security afforded through religious beliefs that many either have avoided in their analytic sessions any reconsideration of such beliefs, or have worked co-operatively with the patient's priest, rabbi or minister, turning over to him the responsibility for helping with religious problems.

Thus, while we may easily discard our fathers' quill pens, their gay waistcoats and their stage coaches, we cling tenaciously to their religious faith. We can alter our houses, our plumbing fixtures, our clothes, our tools, our diets and our ways of travel — and still feel safe. We can, with more difficulty, change our family patterns, our economic and social organization, and our racial attitudes; but to change our religious beliefs touches us at the deepest levels of life and demands profound adjustments, often extremely painful to make. Indeed, rightly or wrongly, most people, as individuals or collectively in religious societies, think it is an important matter what they believe.

So-called "religious liberals" have sometimes been disparaged because it has been said that they think it does not matter much what one believes. They seem to spend so much of their vital enthusiasms in protesting against those beliefs which they regard as false — it is sometimes said — that they have left their people without any constructive faith. Because such groups have not required a statement of belief for acceptance in their societies, it has been assumed that what their members individually believe is after all of small consequence. In fact, this criticism has sometimes been justified. Some liberal societies have avoided public discussions of their differing beliefs. Indeed, freedom in belief presents a serious problem to those to whom religious beliefs are important. Can our religious beliefs continue to be of vital concern to us while at the same time we try to cultivate tolerance of opposing beliefs and appreciation of a variety of points of view? Can it matter to the individual which beliefs he holds, while at the same time he feels no concern for what his neighbors and friends believe? A refusal to delve beneath or behind activities and deeds in order to recognize the ideas, the thinking, the beliefs that motivate those activities surely is superficial. How can worth-while doing and living come without worth-while thinking and believing?

One of England's distinguished religious liberals, Dr. John Macmurray, wrote these words during World War II: "The decay of religious beliefs and the decline of religious influence in the heart of Christian civilization is the major tragedy of our time. For those who have the eyes to look beyond the moment of immediate action it overshadows the tragedy of war, which is indeed one of its most terrifying expressions. . . . For the making and the remaking of any society and especially of a new and wider society is a religious task, and without religion it is quite impossible."[2]

If, then, religious beliefs are regarded as being of such great significance by large numbers of adults in our society, at how early an age are children influenced by the beliefs of their parents? In a society where people of differing faiths meet shoulder to shoulder in daily living, how are our children being affected? How much freedom shall they be given to choose between the alternatives which the presence of different sects and religions suggests? Shall we continue to segregate our children in our different denominational and sectarian camps in order to assure ourselves that at least our own kin will accept our own special inheritance of faith? Or does a culture in which multiple religious systems are actively present require a radically different approach to the religious nurture of youth from the usual way of propaganda? What is it that is important in one's religious beliefs? Is it their likeness to tradition or their harmony with the discoverable nature of human existence? Is it the degree to which beliefs develop a firm conscience, or a "Christian" stereotype for living, or is it the degree to which the children's beliefs encourage wise, warm and socially expanding attitudes? Is the diversity of faiths within our culture something to be tolerated, from which our children must be protected until they are well indoctrinated by us, or does the new world community of which we dream, where different religious groups will live in close communication with one another, require a fundamentally new approach to the religious guidance of the oncoming generation? Must we continue to compete with one another for the loyalties of our children to our own favored religious society? Must we continue to stand each behind his own sectarian fence, waving his own flag of "truth" before the eyes of youth, each shouting his conviction that he has the best? Or have we an obligation to learn somehow ways by which we may all join together in a common search for beliefs of even greater worth than any one group has inherited?

These are but a few among the many questions which we shall be considering in this book. Before we go further, however, let us pause to clarify what we mean by these words, "religious beliefs," "religion," and "faith." Just what is a "re-

ligious belief"? Do we mean merely, or primarily, those
beliefs that center around such ideas as God, prayer, the
Bible, Jesus, salvation, eternity, the supernatural and the
moral law? Where does one draw the line between the secular
and the religious? Are all one's beliefs religious?   -

*From the point of view of this study, one's religious "belief"
or one's "religion" is the "gestalt" of all his smaller specific
beliefs. One's faith is the philosophy of life that gathers up
into one emotional whole — and sometimes, although rarely,
into a reasoned whole — all the specific beliefs one holds
about many kinds of things in many areas of life.*

For example, one of the most important of man's beliefs
is what he thinks about himself. "What a man thinks of himself, that it is which determines, or rather, indicates his
fate."[3] This is one of Henry Thoreau's great insights, now
confirmed by modern psychology. Few, however, think of
belief in oneself as a religious belief. Yet it is like the main
stem out of which the body of one's faith must grow. And what
a person believes about himself depends on what he believes
about his mother and his father, his brothers and his sisters.
And what he believes about these persons in his intimate family influences what he believes about his neighbors and others
in his larger world. And all these beliefs, one by one, grow
up together with his beliefs about all sorts of things: his beliefs about his food, clothes, body, work and play; his beliefs
about birds, fishes, animals, bugs and even dirt; his beliefs
about the earth, rain, winds, the dark and the stars. All these
in time become linked with what he believes about Negroes
and whites, about Communists and Democrats, about rich
and poor, about the strong and the weak, about what is good
and what is bad. All these and unnumbered other beliefs go
into the caldron of experience, together with ideas of God,
prayer, the Bible, Jesus, Moses and eternity. It is quite impossible to separate these beliefs into two kinds, secular and

religious. To the extent that any one of these beliefs affects the quality of the "gestalt" or total configuration of belief, it is religious.

What then is it that is most significant about the total pattern of one's religion? Surely it is not its conformity to Christianity or Judaism, its likeness to Buddhism or Mohammedanism. Its significance must be found at a deeper level where universal truth and universal human need are found.

As a simple introduction to the complexity of the problems involved, let us stop to meditate on a few actual experiences which we have known children to have. These illustrations may indicate the need to raise such questions. They may also suggest other serious issues which should be our concern. At least through a few brief imaginative contacts we may be better able to identify ourselves with children of today and feel with them in their confusions.

A friend was driving three young children to a week-day nursery school. They ranged in age from four and a half to five. Laura's family was Presbyterian; Geoffrey's was Episcopalian; and Dottie's was Unitarian. The three children sat together in the back seat, apparently quite unaware of a listening adult.

Laura had in her hand a colored postcard on which was a rather unusual picture of Jesus as a child. With pride she held it out for the others to see. "Guess what this is a picture of." Since no one quickly volunteered an answer, she gave a hint. "It's someone in heaven!" This started the following conversation:

Dottie: "Let me see that picture. . . . It's not in heaven."

Geoffrey: "It it's in heaven it must be God."

Laura: "No, it's not God."

Dottie: "Of course, it's not God. You can't take a picture of God."

Laura: "Well this isn't God, but it's . . . he's in heaven though."

Finally, since none of the others spoke up, Laura said rapturously, "It's Jesus!"

Dottie: "But Jesus is dead."

Laura: "Yes, but this is his picture. And now he's in heaven."

Geoffrey: "Jesus is not dead!"

Laura: "Yes, Jesus is dead, but he's up in heaven with God now."

Geoffrey: "Jesus is not dead!"

Laura: "Yes, Jesus is dead. He's very, very dead. He died a long time ago."

Geoffrey: "Jesus is not dead!"

Dottie: "Jesus is so dead, Geoffrey. Everybody has to die sometime. You'll die sometime. So will I. So will Laura. Everybody. My grandfather died, so did my grandmother, and they were buried in the ground. Only I still remember them."

Laura: "They're in heaven, I guess. When people die they go to heaven."

Dottie: "How do you know, Laura?"

Geoffrey: "It says so in the Bible."

Dottie: "Well I don't know about that, but I do know that everything dies sometime, even trees, even flowers — everything! Only one thing doesn't ever die. That's *love!* I still love my grandfather and he died. And I even love my grand-mother and she died before I was born. I love her anyway. She was my mummy's mother. We can still remember people and love them when they are dead. The love part doesn't die."

The children then dropped into quietness. Presently they were climbing out of the car and running toward the school building.

Whatever one may think of the comparative worth of the several beliefs which these young children had already appropriated and made their own, it is clear that the beliefs seemed important to the children. Their parents' feelings about them had been contagious, and already these young children were defending their several beliefs against revision. What they had come to believe about Jesus and God and heaven had already become a part of what they believed about themselves and all living things, about life and death.

Margaret's problem was of a different sort. Her mother had given her five-year-old daughter a simple form of Christian instruction. She had told her Bible stories of Jesus and of God, and she had taught her to pray.

One morning Margaret was swinging in the church school playground, pushing the swing higher and higher. So confident was she that she did not even hold onto the rope as she was swinging. "Margaret," called the teacher in charge, "you had better hold onto the ropes or you will fall." But Margaret called back, "O no, I don't need to hold the ropes. I am not afraid to go high, high, high! Jesus will not let me fall." The amazed teacher repeated her warning, but the child gleefully repeated her song: "Jesus will not let me fall."

In a few minutes the child did fall. Bewildered, she pulled herself up from the ground, rubbed her scratched arm, and ran over to the teacher. She held out her arm, asking mutely for a little sympathy. "Anyway, I didn't cry!" she muttered.[4]

It was fortunate that Margaret's experience did not result in any real physical injury. It is more difficult to measure the impact of the emotional shock she felt when she discovered that the basis on which she had built her courage was false to reality. There was no Jesus available to do for her what she had been led to believe he could do.

John, at the age of eight, suffered a similar devastating disillusionment. He was standing on the wharf at a summer swimming place. Children around him were diving into the deep water. John had not learned to swim, but he was secretly confident that he could do so. Had he not been told the story of Jesus' walking on the water, and how Peter had been lifted up when he began to sink? Had not the teacher said that Jesus was always ready to help us if we prayed to him in time of trouble? John needed help at this particular time, so he prayed with all his heart and dived into the water, even before his mother could stop him.

After the boy was rescued and realized what had happened to him, he stood up and stamped his foot angrily. "They lied to me in Sunday school!" he exclaimed. "They said that if I prayed, Jesus would always help me, and he didn't! They lied! I won't ever go to Sunday school again!"

John's violent and angry reaction to what seemed to him a clear-cut deception closed the emotional door of his mind to any contact with the church for months afterwards.

Neither the mother in the first instance, nor the teacher in the second, ever intended to teach these children the beliefs they came to have. They had told the children Bible stories of God's miraculous dealings with people of long ago, and had presented Jesus as living and available today to give support in the same supernatural ways he was reported to have used in Palestine. The children's interpretations of the adult instruction were reasonable from the children's point of view. But when tested, the reality of these beliefs proved to be contrary to the nature of life. This was a truly serious matter to both of these children, for they had taken the teachings of their parents and teachers seriously, and had applied them logically to their immediate situations. Had the children not been helped later to a sounder understanding and hence to other beliefs, their attitudes might have been poisoned for years to come.

Eight-year-old Jimmie fortunately had quite a different experience. For a long time he had felt frustrated because for some vague reason he had not learned to read. His slowness was so marked in contrast to the skill of the other children in his class that Jimmie felt disgraced. His teacher finally

decided to give him special attention for a while. She worked
with him alone on one specific bit of reading until he felt
confident of himself. Then he was given an opportunity to
read this small section in a public program given by the class.
Jimmie did so well in this instance that the other children
recognized his achievement and complimented him. "Why,
you can read well!" "Who said you couldn't read?" "You're
a good reader, Jimmie!" The boy's feeling of personal worth
grew rapidly.

That night before going to bed, he was saying his prayer
as usual: "Now I lay me down to sleep. Bless Papa and Mama
and Auntie." He stopped. Usually he went on to say, ". . . and
help Jimmie to be a good boy." His mother waited. "And . . .
and . . ." she started to prompt him. Finally came the words
from Jimmie himself: "Help me." But then he stopped, and
lifted himself from his knees. "I guess I won't say that to-
night. Jimmie has done pretty good all by himself today."

During that memorable day, Jimmie had discovered a new
feeling about himself, and this discovery led him to change
his belief about prayer and his conception of his relationship
to God. He also found a new meaning in the words "being
good" over which he could really be pleased. This discovery
changed Jimmie's whole pattern of emotional need. This new
belief was neither Presbyterian nor Episcopalian. It was
neither Unitarian nor Catholic. No teacher had taught the
boy his new belief. He had found it for himself, and in this
experience his selfhood had expanded and his hopes had been
energized. Jimmie's changed belief in himself was a religious
experience.

When then we think of the "beliefs" we yearn for children
to have, let us not first ask, "How can I tell my child about
God?" Let us consider rather the many smaller experiences
through which the child is slowly gathering his childlike
philosophy of living. What a child believes really matters,
but the things that matter most do not lie on the surface, in

words said or in prayers repeated. They are found in the "inner world of childhood" where only the sensitive adult may enter.

Some beliefs are like pleasant gardens with high walls around them. They encourage exclusiveness, and the feeling of being especially privileged.
Other beliefs are expansive and lead the way into wider and deeper sympathies.

Some beliefs are like shadows, darkening children's days with fears of unknown calamities.
Other beliefs are like the sunshine, blessing children with the warmth of happiness.

Some beliefs are divisive, separating the saved from the unsaved, friends from enemies.
Other beliefs are bonds in a universal brotherhood, where sincere differences beautify the pattern.

Some beliefs are like blinders, shutting off the power to choose one's own direction.
Other beliefs are like gateways opening up wide vistas for exploration.

Some beliefs weaken a child's selfhood. They blight the growth of resourcefulness.
Other beliefs nurture self-confidence and enrich the feeling of personal worth.

Some beliefs are rigid, like the body of death, impotent in a changing world.
Other beliefs are pliable, like the young sapling, ever growing with the upward thrust of life.

It is indeed important what mankind has believed.
It is important what we believe.
And what a child believes is also a serious matter — not a subject for jest or sentimentality.

2

It Matters How We Gain Our Beliefs

> Nothing is so voluntary an affair as religion, in which,
> if the mind of the worshiper is averse to it, it is already
> destroyed and is no religion.
>
> — LACTANTIUS

THE RELIGIOUS BELIEFS which an individual makes his own
undoubtedly influence his character development. But of even
more profound influence than the beliefs themselves are the
ways through which beliefs are acquired. It is here that the
really vital issue is joined between the major divergent groups
in religious education.

In one group religion is considered as something *given* to
an individual by an authority other than himself, by an authority coming from the past — from revelation, from an inspired
book, from a divine person, or from a divinely ordained
church. Thus religion becomes a body of "affirmations" presented as "truths" to be understood, appreciated and accepted.
When personally accepted, these "truths" become the object
of one's faith and the focus of one's devotion. Certainty regarding such "truths" is thought to be especially important
for young children who are considered incapable of thinking
for themselves about such vital and difficult matters, yet who
need the security that certainty can bring. It is said that their
inborn but undeveloped consciences need to be empowered to
choose the "good" rather than the "evil." By religion pro-
mulgated in this way characters are indeed molded.

The other group holds a less common and sharply different

15

conception of religious development. For them beliefs regarding the universe and man's destiny in it should be the products of maturing emotional experiences, meditation and critical thought, and not assumptions with which to begin. Religion is, therefore, not a heritage which the child has a God-given right to receive, not something to be imparted to him by a teacher or a group. Rather it is regarded as a vital and healthy result of his own creative thought and feeling and experience as he responds to life in all its fullness.

Such a religion will develop slowly. The initial steps are largely emotional, exploratory and unorganized. Out of these early emotional beginnings the individual formulates a philosophy of life for himself. Influences from without and from the past affect the formation of such a religion; but the life-giving element is within the child and in his present experiences. Such a process of achieving religion never ceases. Full maturity is never attained. As the personality grows and changes so do the beliefs grow and change.

Thus we see that in one group religion is conceived of as a heritage received from the past and delivered with the stamp of authority. In the other its inspiration in the beginning and throughout the total span of life arises out of the natural needs and concerns of the individual who seeks a rich and satisfying life.

Although the contrast between these two points of view should not be exaggerated, neither should the difference be regarded lightly. For if one thinks of religion primarily in terms of something created by each individual, the first question to be asked is not: What has religion to give to a child? It is rather: How may a child contribute to his own religious growth? It is not: How does religion influence character development? Instead, the question of first importance is: How does character development influence the kind of religion a child makes his own? How is it possible for a child to build his own religion? Only when we understand the child's potentialities can we understand how we, his elders, may help or hinder him in gradually assuming responsibility for forming his religion.

Not only does the point of view one takes on this major issue determine the starting point, but also it affects continually the very nature of the processes of religious guidance, the goals sought, and the emotional atmosphere that is maintained between adults and children.

Since the conception of religion as a gift coming from the past to be handed on from one generation to another is such a dominant one in our society, it is important that we examine more carefully the effect of this point of view on the methods by which children have been taught religion, and the results that have accrued from it.

Ever since our forefathers first established our democracy on this continent, it has been assumed that each particular group or sect in our society should be responsible for transmitting its own religion to its own children. Each group, believing that it has the best to give, musters all its efforts to impart with persuasive power that which it proclaims as the truth. The attempt is made openly, and with general approval, to bind young children by personal loyalty to the religion of their fathers and to hold them in later life within the religious fold into which they were born.

In this approach, therefore, the beliefs characterizing each particular group are given a large emphasis in work with children. These beliefs are of two types, those that express the nature of God and man's obligations to him, and those which indicate what is "right" and what is "wrong" in man's conduct toward his fellow men. Of these two types, the beliefs pertaining to the existence and nature of God have usually been regarded in our Western culture as primary, and those pertaining to man's duty to man as secondary, being derived from a belief in God. The lack of belief in a God who ordains righteousness is commonly blamed for juvenile delinquency, the materialism of our civilization, and many other social evils.

This emphasis on belief in God is found in most Christian and Jewish literature for young children. The existence of God is assumed, however, rather than made the object of thoughtful study. Children are not expected to ask *why* people have believed that God is a reality. His existence and his attributes are taken for granted. Not only is God assumed, but the general system of moral ideas embodied in the Christian and Jewish heritage is also assumed as true and "good." God rewards the "good" and punishes the "bad." Bible characters in most of the Bible story books for children are either men who obeyed God's voice and were rewarded, or who disobeyed and were punished. The fact that young children have so little in their own experience by which to judge critically what they are told is regarded usually as an asset. The early years are golden ones for such indoctrination.

In common practice this emphasis is revealed in a type of reasoning such as this: A small child cannot grasp an abstract or cosmic thought of God. Since, however, "goodness" and "love" are the most important aspects in "our best thought of God," the God idea is made personal and concrete for the child. In Christian circles young children are told stories of Jesus as a man who was especially kind to children and to all people in trouble. Then it is explained that Jesus is like God, and that God is like Jesus; indeed, that the two are one and the same.

God is commonly spoken of in religious literature as a "loving Heavenly Father," who is different from flesh-and-blood fathers since he is invisible, and his permanent home is "heaven," a place vaguely located above the earth. This "Heavenly Father," although far away, is always near by. He loves children and guards them so they need never be afraid; however, he expects a great deal of children in return for his love. He likes a "good" and "kind" child. He does not like "bad" children. Indeed, in much common conversation between parents and children regarding God, he is presented as prepared to inflict punishments on those who disobey their parents, or who tell a lie. Bible stories are read or told to young children in order that such beliefs and ideas of right and wrong may be made more impressive. Although some of the stories told contain accounts of miraculous happenings which the parents or teachers themselves no longer regard as records of facts, yet the children are told these stories because they are in the Scriptures, and because the children enjoy hearing them.

Let us examine the soundness of this point of view. What are the natural consequences in the emotional and intellectual development of the child?

To most children under six the world is filled with wonders for which they can give no reasonable explanation. Fairies, Santa Claus, witches, a snake that can talk, a man who can dam up the waters of a big sea merely by a command, are all believable. The story of angels singing in the sky over the birth of a baby is a wonderful fantasy for the child who has been told nothing about his own birth. A little child can imagine people being made well by a few spoken words. He can ask in prayer for a play-train and believe that God can produce the train in some magic way. Does the child himself not perform magic whenever he turns off the electric light or starts the radio by a twist of the fingers? To imagine the dead able to come back to life is a common fantasy among young children. Stories and tales of wonder are found in every religious culture, and are passed on to children as a part of their religious heritage. It is thought that to know the stories will in some way help to develop reverence, and will impress on children the desirability of pleasing God.

If these stories are told concretely in such a way that a young child can imagine the characters as real people in his present experience, and if he can identify himself emotionally with them, such methods may have great influence. But the question that should concern us is: What is the nature of the influence? Will the child as a result of his faith in God feel more truly secure in his world or will his reasons for fear be increased? If a child looks upon floods, sickness, defeat in war, or death as forms of divine punishment (as they are so often presented in Biblical stories), will the fear of such punishments increase his desire or his power to be "good"? Or will the already rebellious child find a divine sanction for his own acts of aggression against those he dislikes? Will such stories give a child a sound understanding of his own capacities or will they tend to foster an illusion of strength by encouraging the expectation of some "special providence"? Will some children decide, as John did, that they too can walk on water or do other impossible things because they have accepted seriously the assurance of Jesus' power to save? Or will Jesus simply become another superman in their worlds of fantasy?

We do not doubt that the telling of Bible stories does mold the thinking and feelings of young children. Our concern is with the quality of the results. In just what ways are children being influenced? What kinds of emotional needs are being satisfied? Is the child's belief in magic being prolonged and his growing-up retarded? Or do such methods really sharpen his interest in the real nature of the universe and so help him to grow toward maturity? Our experience has led to the conclusion that there are much more promising ways of introducing young children to religious feelings and beliefs than through the early use of Bible-story books.

A second common way of introducing children to religion, one that is equally authoritarian in type, is the way that approaches beliefs indirectly through induction into religious ceremonials. Little emphasis is given at first to the beliefs implicit in these ceremonials. In such groups, children are taught to say the words of prayers and to perform acts in the ceremonials before the ideas can be explained to them, and sometimes almost before they can pronounce the words right. Thus religion becomes, not so much a set of beliefs to be upheld and accepted, as a pattern of group ceremonials into which the child needs to be habit-trained. Religion becomes something to be acted out in group rituals. Certain words are to be said, certain postures taken, a certain vocabulary made familiar. It is assumed the children in later years will clothe the forms with meanings. In this kind of religious education religion becomes a set of habit patterns to be followed, like the daily bath or the rules of polite society.

What happens then in the immediate life experiences of children so guided? Finding enjoyment in performing acts for which the child can see no clear reason must lead him to focus attention on adult approval and the pleasure of formal participation rather than on the meanings beneath these externals. Surely neither words nor acts that are without meaning to a child can really nourish his life. This is an effective method of tying children emotionally to their particular cultural patterns, without their feeling a need to examine the reasons for such patterns.

And what happens to the child as the years move on, as he finds that other groups have different ceremonies and believe differently? He cannot but equate the external words and rituals with his religion. If he does so, then religion becomes something that separates one group from another, rather than something that binds humanity together by means of deeply felt universal experiences underneath varying forms. Furthermore, children so taught will tend to think of religion as something unique to their particular ethnic group, something inherited from their particular ancestors and peculiar to their culture. Their own religion will naturally seem the best. Such children are likely to feel no more responsibility for the nature of their religion than they feel for the lands and money they may inherit. The child will discover that he is a Methodist or a Baptist, a Mohammedan or a Roman Catholic, a follower of Judaism or of Buddha, just as he discovers that he has Nordic or Negro or Asiatic features. To question or to reject such a religion is like rejecting one's own kin.

One or the other of these two ways, either of indoctrination in beliefs or of habit-training in ceremonials, or both of them combined, has been the time-honored way of educating the young in practically every great religious culture. Religious education is still predominantly of these two types. Such an education comes to the children primarily from the outside. It is given by means of external authority, the authority either of an assumed creed or of an inherited custom.

These methods of passing on the heritage were developed first in societies that were totalitarian in their political and social structures. It was natural that these methods should have been used in societies where the right to rule was inherited and in which the great majority of the people were expected to be ignorant and obedient, but do these authoritarian methods fit a dynamic democratic society?

We must return to our primary inquiry indicated at the beginning of this chapter. How much difference does it make *how* a child comes by his beliefs? Is the *how* as significant as the *what?* Suppose a child is led to feel that he ought to believe what he hears because the Bible tells him so; or suppose he is encouraged to question the standards of long ago and the ways people used to think of God, asking why they felt as they did and why today some people feel and think differently: how much difference will these two ways of dealing with ideas and practices make in the child's personality development? Are the results in a child's character when he is encouraged to carry responsibility for his own thoughts different from the results obtained when he is led to feel that the best thinking has already been done for him or that to be a Christian he *should* believe thus and so? Does teaching religious beliefs and ceremonials authoritatively, or with certainty assumed, tend to develop children who are themselves authoritative, holding positive and unchanging convictions? Does the opposite approach tend to encourage a more flexible type of personality? Which type seems to us to promise the greater usefulness in our time?

The results of a recent extensive piece of research made by Dr. Else Frenkel-Brunswick and her associates are enlightening at this point.[1] They studied 1500 children of varying socio-economic backgrounds and ranging in age from eleven to sixteen. Out of this number 120 were chosen for detailed study. One half of this smaller group were chosen because they were found to be extremely prejudiced against those who differed from them. The other half were chosen because they were the children who showed the smallest number of such prejudices. The results of the study of these two types can be summed up briefly.

It was found that the children in the more prejudiced group had been educated for the most part in home, school and church by authoritarian methods; while the other group had been nurtured in what the author of the study characterizes as a "liberal" manner. Their parents had been more permissive, democratic and flexible in their controls and had given their children more responsibility in the forming of their ideals and beliefs.

The children who had been accustomed to authoritarian controls were already becoming authoritarian in their attitudes toward others. Having been obliged to accept conformity for themselves, they demanded it of others also. They seemed to need inflexible rules to follow, not only in morals but in many other areas also. Rigidity was already tending to become a pervasive trait. This group had "an exaggerated social-status concern." Outward appearances were important in determining values. These children seemed to need approval for themselves in order to maintain their security, and they tended to condemn those whose ways were different. They had great admiration for the strong, the tough and the powerful, and at the same time they had only contempt for the weak. They showed "a generalized rejection of all that was weak and different." They were most at ease when they could make their value judgments in terms of white and black or "good" and "bad." Their repressed resentments toward authority "seemed to be displaced upon socially inferior and foreign groups." "Behind a rigid façade of conformity," there seemed to be an "underlying fascination in the thought of chaos and destruction." Inhibited in their desire for independence, they were found to seek rough games and other forms of explosive outlets for their hostilities. Furthermore, this group were less scientifically oriented than the other group. They could accept more easily superstitious ideas and "chance" as explanations of situations they could not readily understand.

On the other hand, the group of children who had lived in "liberal" homes where controls were less rigid and ideas were subjected to reasonable examination were found to be more tolerant of differences and more able to maintain an "equalitarian and individualized approach to people" of different types. They took "internal values" more seriously than "external appearances." Both groups had hostilities and anxieties, but the "liberal" children could talk over their feelings more freely. They could "express disagreement with, and resentment against, parents more openly." They "spoke less often of strictness and harshness when telling of their fathers" and more often "in terms of companionship." They were "more oriented toward love and less toward power." "They more often employed the help of adults in working out their own problems of sex and aggression." They were "more flexible and less likely to form stereotyped opinions of others." They were better able to "incorporate the values of society." They were scientifically better oriented, more able to withstand "hateful propaganda" both in the forms of "defamation

of minorities and of glorification of war." Being better able
to integrate their instinctual drives into their total consciousness, they were able to be more creative and more open to
new ideas.

The results of this study are indeed a grave challenge to
the prevailing practice of propagating religious beliefs and of
fostering religious ceremonials mainly by assuming or affirming their rightness. The study strongly suggests that not only
is it important *what* children believe, but that it is even more
significant *how* they develop their beliefs. Both of these
groups of children studied were for the most part from so-
called Christian homes. Presumably many of the same general
ideas had been taught them. The marked difference in the
personality outcomes must have been brought about primarily
by the ways in which the children and their ideas were
treated. In general, the authoritarian way had led to the
development of authoritarian personalities. The democratic
and reasonable way had led to the development of democratic
and reasonable children. In short, beliefs held primarily because they were once revealed, and not because their truth
had been freely examined and personally evaluated, may become a factor in creating just the opposite kinds of attitudes
from those which religious leaders usually mean to inculcate.
The study, therefore, leads to the conclusion that it is of the
greatest significance *how* beliefs are gained.

Under the methods of propaganda and authoritative teaching, the creative springs of religious thinking slowly dry up.
The accent on fixed and unchangeable patterns congeals
thought. Creative religion has been dependent on the emergence of individuals or groups who could face directly for
themselves the problems of existence, who penetrated courageously the forms and rituals, who believed the truth had
not been finally delivered. Creative religion is dependent
on those who are not afraid to say, "It was said by them of
old time . . . but I say unto you." The authoritarian or gift-

giving way of religious guidance may be a way of insuring the maintenance of the *status quo;* it is *not* the way of creative growth and change.

An illustration may give clarity to the distinction between these two approaches to religious guidance. It shows the effect on a young mind of the authoritarian approach. It suggests also the creative possibilities in a free attitude.

Five-year-old Jill had been the object of a certain amount of indoctrination, not from her father or mother, and not so much from her church, but from a playmate who had been the object of some successful indoctrination.

Jill and her mother were mending clothes together one day. Jill was choosing colors for her dolls' dresses. The two began to talk about how colors made them feel.

"White is God's color," said Jill, "but I guess he likes pink too, it's so pretty. He likes blue too. He made the sky all blue and blue. But he doesn't like brown. It's Nazi color. I don't like it either. Yellow is Jap's color. I wish God liked yellow. It's nice. It's like laughing. But it's Jap's color. God wouldn't like Jap's color. Japs are bad. They kill people."

The mother, startled by these remarks, asked Jill why she thought in these ways. "Joan told me," Jill explained. "God is all white all over. Brown is for Nazis. Yellow is for Japs. It's a good thing she told me. I didn't know."

The mother suggested that sunshine is yellow. "It shines on the Japanese as well as on us. Don't you think the sun belongs to God?"

But Jill repeated her stereotyped answers. The mother lit her cigarette and sat in silence trying to think of a better angle of approach.

"That smoke is blue!" pondered Jill. "Joan said smoke is gray."

"Joan doesn't seem to notice things for herself very much," said the mother. "She just listens to what other people say. You *do* notice things for yourself. You learned something about smoke just now that Joan doesn't know. *You will have to learn to notice for yourself what belongs to God."*

"But," said Jill, "I can't notice God. I can't see him. I don't know anything about him."

"You can see the part of the world that is around you," said the mother. *"What you see is part of what God does.* People have learned all of what we know about God by seeing for themselves what is in his world. If you just listen to other people you will never know any more about God than they have noticed. If you learn for yourself you will be helping us all to know more about God."[2]

Jill had indeed been noticing many things for herself, but the idea that her own experiences had any connection with "God" gave her a new outlook. She had supposed that since she could not see God she had no way of finding out about him. She had already felt a conflict between her own thoughts and what Joan had told her. She had wished that God liked yellow, but it had not occurred to her to question Joan's assertions or to ask her how she knew. The mother's life-giving comment, "You will have to learn to notice for yourself what belongs to God," awakened her.

It is to be further noted that these ideas about God which had taken such firm and dogmatic hold upon these two children, Jill and Joan, had probably never been openly expressed by any teacher of religion. The ideas in the minds of the teachers and the impressions received by the children were different ideas. Joan had seen a picture of Jesus in white. She was told that Jesus was God. God must like white. And then the prejudices prevailing during World War II became attached to this basic idea of God. He did not like the Nazis or the Japs, and they were somehow linked with brown and yellow. This sequence of thinking in the mind of a five-year-old is quite logical if considered from the point of view of her experience. The spiritual beliefs which the adult teachers thought they were implanting had been misunderstood; yet all the corollaries derived from the religious indoctrination were believed with the same dogmatic assurance that had marked the first idea given them. Such is the process of degeneration that almost inevitably takes place when an idea too large or too intangible for a child's understanding is inculcated and the child then tries to work it into his real experience.

But Jill was given an enlivening thought. She herself could notice the kind of world that was around her, and from what she found she could draw her own conclusions about God. She might even find something more than had ever been found before by anyone. This gave the child respect for her own mind and her own feelings. Other conversations followed. Still thinking that the Bible told all about God, she asked to have parts of it read. Although the mother tried to satisfy her daughter and chose with care the parts she read, Jill found herself unable to grasp the meanings, and when she did partly understand she began wondering. Soon she began to distinguish between "the God in the stories" and "the real God." She began to sense a Reality in her own experience — truer to her than any of the symbols of the imagination that the Bible used. Finally, one day she closed a conversation with these words: "Mother, do you think if we could fly out and out, instead of in, past all the sky and where the stars are, that we would come to where there is just God and not any world?"

In this episode we see the two conflicting types of religious guidance impinging on two children. Joan apparently had already been won by an authoritarian approach. Jill was struggling: her mind had been almost subdued by the power of such a religion, even though transmitted to her largely through a playmate of her own age. Fortunately her mother opened a window to the light. "Notice for yourself. You can see as well as anybody." And Jill began to grow in spiritual stature. From then on she became an original adventurer.

Once she realized that God may be found in this realm of present living, Jill grew in her awareness of the great ineffable Mystery, which she came to call "the real God."

Thus we have contrasted two ways by which children may acquire their beliefs. One is the way of receiving and accepting what has been "said by them of old"; the other is the way of thinking things out for oneself. One way begins with the past and with authority; the other begins with the present and with experience. One begins with the stories of great people whose lives are to be imitated; the other begins with the child himself and his companions who have their own conflicts to solve. One begins with the presentation of ideals and principles to be followed; the other is based on the belief that learning how to live a good life is a matter for experimentation and discovery. One encourages discipleship; the other encourages adventuring beyond the authorities of old, seeking ever richer insights.

The second of these two ways has been little tried in any religious culture. Indeed, it has seldom even been conceived of as desirable. It is based on the belief that living forms cannot be passed on from generation to generation merely by attempts to preserve the fruits. Fruits to be preserved must be put in cold storage or dried or become fossilized. It is only when the fruits are cut open and the living seeds are freed from the old matrix and then planted in new soil that living and continuing forms are made possible.

This less-tried way rests on the assumption that belief in God is not a simple item of knowledge to be handed from one person to another. God cannot be seen or touched or located or proved as a single fact. In God are gathered up all facts, all knowledge, all experiences, all thoughts, all feelings. To simplify is to belittle God. Vital religion lives in the totality of experiences — not merely in words said, or in ceremonies performed, or in ideas affirmed.

This way, less often tried, is not easy. Radical changes

in adult experiencings, feelings and thinking are needed. New meanings are required for these old words — "religion," "faith," "belief." New techniques in guiding children's development through direct experiencing are involved. Is the new way practical? Is it realistic? What results have followed when it has been tried? Much careful experimenting is needed far beyond anything as yet even conceived. We are still in the pioneering stage. We have the written records of but a small number of teachers who have been venturing. Selections from such records are interspersed throughout this book in order to give reality to the philosophy. These have been set forth alongside some of the recent findings presented by scientifically oriented students of childhood. These experiences are recorded not as proofs, but rather as hints of things to come.

Since the very earliest steps during the first four or five years of life are the most significant, we shall devote the two following chapters to what we have been learning about the child's potential religious development during these earliest years.

3

Natural Beginnings in Early Childhood

Man is born with rainbows in his heart
And you'll never read him unless you consider the rainbows.
— CARL SANDBURG

ONE SUNDAY MORNING a professor from a foreign country
was visiting a class of junior high school boys and girls in the
Riverside Church, New York City. When the class hour was
nearly over the teacher asked the visitor if he would say a few
words. In response he told of his keen interest in all he had
heard, but he said: "This is all very different from the way
we do in my country. There we teach the boys and girls the
Catechism."

"What is that?" asked one of the class.

The surprised professor repeated some of the questions and
answers in the Shorter Catechism of the Presbyterian Church
to explain to these uninformed Americans methods used in
the Old World. When he had finished one of the boys said
thoughtfully: "Professor, that is perhaps all very well in your
country, but it wouldn't work with us. It seems to me you are
setting up a kind of ladder, but it has only one rung and that's
at the top. It's all right if you can reach that far."

This expression of insight coming from an adolescent boy
highlights the contrast between a possible natural way of
religious development and one of the traditional ways of religious education. But what *is* a more natural way? What
are the first steps like? How can a little child begin to be
religious naturally without being instructed in the religious
beliefs of his parents? At how early an age are these natural

31

steps taken? And how may teachers and parents encourage or discourage young children as they take these natural steps? To help answer these questions let us examine in some detail why a natural way of religious growth seems possible.

While many religious leaders have assumed that they knew by dogma the nature of the newborn baby, modern psychologists and pediatricians have been studying babies and small children in order to find out what they are actually like. Fifty years of research and scientific experimentation have yielded a great deal of new understanding. These findings have revolutionized the theory and practice of child care, resulting in the creation of the modern profession of pediatrics. These findings have also changed the habits and attitudes of thousands of parents in their dealings with babies and children in their homes. Although it must be said that few of these scientific studies have included any direct examination of the young child's religious development, nevertheless the conclusions from the studies are not unrelated to religion as we understand it, and their implications have begun to affect in small ways the procedures of religious leaders in their work with young children. Unfortunately, however, ecclesiastical leaders have put barriers in the way of forthright use of these findings of psychology and medicine so that religious education in large measure is still based on assumptions about babies and children that are quite out of keeping with these recent findings.

What then are these important findings regarding young children that need serious consideration? Although these are many and complex, yet a few major conclusions can be stated which will suggest the direction in which psychological thinking with regard to very young children is moving. The first of these is this: a young baby is an emotionally dynamic person, already strongly motivated to struggle for what is most important to his development. A new baby is not a creature who can be easily influenced or molded into a pattern other than that which he himself desires. A baby's emotions are all-absorbing and a more decisive factor for or against his health and growth than any other of the usual variables in his physical care.

It is through his feelings that a young baby finds his major contacts with the world outside himself. Unable to focus his eyes, he sees only a big blur of light and shadow. Unable to locate sounds, he hears noises coming from everywhere. Unable to sit or roll over or even to turn his head, unable to use his hands or his feet, unable to communicate except by crying into the vagueness around him, not yet knowing what is within him and what is without, the newborn baby would seem to be completely helpless. But actually he is far from helpless, for he has a dynamic quality in his personality that compels him to struggle for the satisfaction of his basic needs. The very forcefulness of his emotional nature is his protection, and his ways of calling for help are irresistible to the normal adult.

The newborn baby is not only a forceful individual, he is also very sensitive to the emotional atmosphere around him. He is quick to feel what is detrimental and what is satisfying. This emotional sensitivity is evident even during the very first moments after birth, when he seems to feel keenly the danger that threatens him in being separated from his mother's body. The newborn child senses so keenly the seriousness of the first few hours and days of life that it requires several weeks for most babies to relax and smile and to begin actively to enjoy living.

What is the most dominant and important of all the young baby's emotional needs? The psychologists and pediatricians seem agreed that it is the need for love; and being loved is the first step toward learning to trust and then how to love in return. To have this need for love adequately met has been shown to be even more important than having the proper amount and quality of food, or the comforts of a bed or a warm blanket. Physicians have learned by experimentation that if the mother holds her baby in her arms and loves him for awhile even before the umbilical cord is cut, his circulation and breathing are both improved.

Studies have been made of babies who were kept, for one reason or another, in hospitals or institutions beyond the usual ten days after birth, and who were separated from their mothers for several months. It was found that although they were given the very best physical care, they did not gain with the rapidity of normal children who could be near their mothers and be given motherly attention. Those who were returned to the hospital after having had the satisfaction of warm mother love fared the worst. Dr. Rene Spitz[1] and Dr. Margaret Ribble[2] and others found that such children became dull and inattentive to their surroundings. Their general development was slowed down, they became listless or morose, hostile or unco-operative. Dr. Spitz describes their emotional reaction as one of "real grief." Their faces became sad or sullen, they seemed unable to relax, their fists were kept tight. Rather than trying to make contact with people they withdrew from strangers. Some of the babies lost weight, at the period when gain in weight should have been greatest. These symptoms were most marked among children ranging from three months to a year and a half in age.

A two-year-old child who had lost her mother was brought into Johns Hopkins Hospital because her stomach was not retaining its food. The doctor made a careful examination but could discover no cause for the trouble. He diagnosed the case as one of a child needing "love." He wrote the three letters "T. L. C." on her chart. The kind of treatment these letters indicated had become so common in that hospital that the nurse knew at once what was meant: "Tender Loving Care" for fifteen minutes after each feeding.

The nurse in charge reported that if, in her hurry to do other things that seemed more important, she cut short that "fifteen minutes," the child's food would inevitably come up after she had put the baby back in bed. When she kept dutifully to the letter of her instructions and spent the full fifteen minutes with the child in her arms, but still did not feel entirely relaxed, and so was not wholly attentive to the child, the inevitable vomiting would follow. But if, for fifteen minutes, she gave herself to the child, really enjoying her and loving her, the food would invariably stay down.

Similar dramatic episodes have been repeated so often in the experience of pediatricians and nurses that there seems no longer any doubt in their minds that the young child's most vital need is to be loved. But love is not merely another item to be added to the baby's schedule. It is something that should pervade all his care. Nor is the loving he needs merely something he feels with his sense of touch, something which the mother can give by kisses and fondling alone. It *is* that, but it is also something more than that. The baby seems to crave a spontaneous love on an instinctive level of real feeling. Nor is it the immature love of a child for a doll that a human baby wants. It is rather a mature love that strives to support him by meeting his needs, that seeks to respond intelligently to his pleas for help.

A normal baby whose need for this true love is satisfied reacts with growing trust, relaxation and delight. Without this food for his spirit the personality of the child suffers real damage. His growing trust turns to fear. His outgoing interest in the world around him is dulled. His urge for activity is lessened. His desire to make more contacts with others turns to resentment, and his trustful readiness to co-operate changes to rebellion, or to a dulling of his desire to struggle. Such results have been demonstrated so often that pediatricians and psychologists during the last ten years have changed, in radical ways, their methods of child care.

In the second place, modern students of young children not only have developed a deep respect for the inborn nature of a newborn child, but they have come to have an equally profound respect also for the natural schedules according to which the child grows.

A baby, like any other living thing, grows according to a plan which, in some mysterious way, is a part of his very being. During the months before birth each organ in the human fetus has its own special time for developing. If, for some reason, the growth of that organ does not take place when its time comes, it never does grow properly to full maturity. It is permanently disabled or deformed, and the next organ in the order of growth is also adversely affected. All living things seem to have their time schedules prepared, as it were, in advance by some over-ruling Destiny or Power, or by Life itself.

The schedules for physical growth after birth have also been carefully observed. Doctors and educators are being trained to watch for each sign of a child's readiness for the next developmental step. They are taught to note the child's first spontaneous efforts, and to celebrate with him his successes. In short, they wait until the time is ripe to make changes in the child's physical care.

A further discovery of even more vital import has been made. It is now recognized that the young child's schedule for physical and mental development is inescapably conditioned on his emotional growth, and that there is a natural schedule for the emergence of emotions paralleling the schedule for physical and mental development. The growth of mature emotions is conditioned upon the rich development of immature types of emotions belonging primarily in the earlier periods. The schedule for the natural and healthy development of a young child's emotional life during the first four or five years may be roughly outlined.[3]

As has already been pointed out, first appears the emotional *struggle for mother love*. When the baby becomes assured of the reality and constancy of a love that cares for his real needs, then there develops a general feeling of trust, relaxation, and contentment — the beginning of a *faith in life*.

This assurance of love then leads to the beginnings of *an ability to give love* as well as to receive it. There appear spontaneous responses of gladness, and the gentle fondling of the mother's face and breasts.

Following upon this growth in happiness, the child next begins to show a strong *desire to be self-directing*. He wants at times to be independent of adult control, to make some decisions on his own. This urge usually shows itself most vigorously when the baby has learned to move about on his own feet. With the gaining of skill in the use of his larger muscles, the child feels an enlarging vigor. He wishes to prove his power by accomplishing things without any help from outside. He may also need at times to prove his power by refusing to follow adult guidance. This is the usual time for frequent temper tantrums, and these are regarded as normal during the first two or three years. The child is experimenting with his self-direction.

If the external controls are weakened sufficiently to permit frequent successful attempts at self-direction, the child grows in his *feelings of personal worth*. This self-respect in turn makes him feel *safer in co-operating with adult desires*. Feeling that he has once been definitely separated from his parents and has become an individual who can stand on his own feet, he wants to re-establish the feeling of closeness to his parents on a higher level of maturity.

With this step taken, the child is ready to go out into a larger world than that within his own home. He develops an *interest in other children,* and is able to enter into their feelings with some understanding. This development of empathy is impossible, however, until the child has developed some degree of respect for himself. He must be assured that he is liked by his parents before he can wholeheartedly like himself; and he must like himself before he can like other children of his approximate age. Until he has this assurance, he may do kind things for other children under the direction of adults, but he cannot feel kindly toward them. He can share his toys because he is told to do so, but he cannot really be happy about it.

With this mutual receiving and giving of love and kindness, the child is able to move still farther out into a larger world where he meets new people and finds out new things. As his ability to think and to speak grows, an intense *curiosity* naturally develops about almost everything he sees and hears. At this stage the child becomes an eager questioner, not merely because the facts about which he inquires are necessary for him to know, but because he has an *emotional need to feel his relationship to this larger world* he is discovering. He needs to explore, and at the same time he feels the need to maintain his own sense of security. Emotionally he is searching for a philosophy of life — and a philosophy of life is religion. This last stage in the emotional growth of the preschool child we shall consider more at length in the following chapter.

Such a brief outline of a very young child's emotional development is, of course, most inadequate, and its accuracy deserves further examination. None should infer that the process is a simple matter of stepping out of one emotional stage into another, or of giving up one emotion to achieve the next. The process is complex. There is overlapping. All of these basic emotions will continue to be present throughout all of the child's later life. To a greater or less degree they are felt by people of all ages. The important point is that *these emotions emerge for the first time at certain stages in the child's early development.* To expect them before that stage has been reached will lead to disappointment. To discourage their flowering when the time has come for their appearance is to thwart the child's wholesome emotional development, and this may have serious emotional consequences not only in later life, but directly during childhood.

Modern research in child development, then, has much to

teach parents and leaders in church and synagogue. In these short pages only a few hints have been given of these important findings, but the implications that can be drawn even from these alone cut deep into prevailing assumptions and practices in the teaching of religion. Let us note the most outstanding of these challenges.

Modern students of child life do not think of babies as "born in sin," as the prayer book asserts. They do not regard young children as having evil instincts whose expression must be curbed. Many psychologists of young children would not now even say that babies are born morally neutral, with their natures evenly balanced between tendencies on the one hand to be selfish, and tendencies on the other hand to be good. It is now quite generally believed that babies are born conditioned toward the most vital of all the values which high religion has always cherished. "The child is born an activelv co-operating organism."[4] He is conditioned toward love rather than hostility, toward co-operation rather than rebellion. He is born with a natural readiness to respond to love, even with a strong urge to struggle for love if it seems to be denied him. If his desire for love turns to hostility it is not because of a natural propensity for evil, but because he has been deprived of the love which is his natural right. In fact, these untoward emotional attitudes in a baby are danger signals which should tell us the child has been deprived of essential spiritual vitamins.

Speaking in theological terms, what more could a wise Creator do than to give to each newborn child this great yearning for love? How could he make spiritual nurture more natural or more promising? Instead of believing, as our ancestors so long held, that a baby is born with a natural moral handicap, we can now be assured that the scales are definitely weighted in favor of the values that all the great religions of the world have tried to promote in one form or another — namely, love, trust and co-operation.

This scientifically based confidence in the potential goodness of human nature, combined with the equally strong trust in the natural schedule by which all children seem to grow, has led to the promulgation of the so-called "permissive methods" of child care. These are slowly replacing methods of discipline in rigid schedules and rules. This belief in the potential goodness of original nature has taken out the foundation stones from under the theory of discipline for the sake of discipline in character development.

A growing number of pediatricians and psychiatrists believe in letting the young child have his own way (in as large a measure as is consistent with health and safety) because they have actually found by experimentation that the child's way has so often proved to be better than any of the other ways adults had devised. In the Book of Isaiah a prophet proclaimed the coming of the wonderful day when "a little child shall lead them." This prophecy is now being fulfilled in the realm of child care. Scientists of child life are letting the children take the lead, and in so doing they believe they have learned wisdom. Instead of feeling the need to urge the child to conform to their ideals of a good life, these men and women are trying to be sensitive and intelligent when the child tries to express his desires. They are developing ears that hear and eyes that see the unspoken signs. They are seeking to identify their feelings with those of the child, and to satisfy them in ways that will enhance his well-being. In short, they are trying to work with the child rather than assuming there is something evil to work against.

But there still lingers in the unconscious of many adults an unexamined and culturally inherited assumption that what the baby or young child wants is not likely to be good for him. Because of the supposition that a child is born selfish, and that by some kind of discipline this selfishness must be hammered out of him, many are afraid to give the child what he wants when he asks for it lest he develop a selfish character.

When he is grown up he will discover, so it is said, that he cannot have his own way all the time: therefore it is well to begin when he is young to teach him this lesson. In fact, belief in the child's natural evil propensities is still for many leaders the basic reason for having religion at all.

Dr. Charles Aldrich, after his long experience in the Mayo Clinic, summed up his findings regarding "spoiled" children in this manner:

> Every doctor has the opportunity of knowing many such youngsters, but I have never seen one who was spoiled because his parents consistently planned his life to meet his basic needs. In my experience most spoiled children are those who, as babies, have been denied essential gratifications in a mistaken attempt to fit them into a rigid regime. Warmth, cuddling, freedom of action, and pleasant associations with food and sleep have been pushed out of the way to make room for a technique. The lack of these things is so keenly felt by the time babyhood is past that such children have learned their own efficient techniques of whining and tantrums as a means of getting their desires. In this way is fostered the belligerent, fussy, unpleasant personality of the typical "spoiled" child, who insists on undue attention because he has missed this fundamental experience. A satisfied baby does not need to develop these methods of wresting his comforts from an unresponsive world.[5]

Some of the most loving parents seem to be actually afraid of "the child's dynamics," and begin early to plan ways by which they can subdue him. The presence of this assumed but unexamined dogma in our society that "man is born in sin" lies dormant in our cultural "unconscious" and before we are fully aware of what we are doing it rises up to influence us to take on the role of disciplinarian with our children. The dogma, although no longer overtly accepted, has left a feeling tone in its wake which gives us an exaggerated sense of responsibility for teaching children to follow the "good." Some of us perhaps find that to play the role of disciplinarian meets our own emotional needs; or we may not yet be entirely emancipated from our own feelings of personal weakness that were caused by our resentments against the arbitrary controls exerted on us during childhood. We, therefore, in turn, have a compulsion to show our strength and superiority over our own children.

There is also another reason found in the nature of our Western culture which affects us all. We are living in a civilization, as Dr. Erik Erikson says, which accents efficiency, where time is money and "calls for orderliness, punctuality, and thrift. . . ." "We have assumed that a child is an animal which must be broken or a machine which must be set and tuned—while in fact, human virtues can grow only by steps."[6] This machine-age atmosphere brings pressure on all of us to hurry, and we find ourselves demanding efficiency even in a small child's behavior. He must be taught bowel control as early as possible because mother needs to be saved the labor of washing diapers. He must be kept quiet and confined in a playpen because the adults in the house are annoyed by a runabout at play, or the room arrangements will be untidied. The child must eat all the special foods the doctor or the radio advertisement prescribes as good for him because a parent wants his child to be grade "A." He must be put to bed regularly because everyone else in the household wants a free evening. So "habit training" begins, and the child who yields to parental demands is called "good," and the one who rebels is called "naughty." We are in such a hurry to make our children into the latest model that we are prone to forget the emotional accompaniments that may be brought by our discipline. An outward control is then easily substituted for a dynamic inner control. In short, we are in a hurry and the quickest way seems to be by command, accented by the threat of punishment or by words of reproof.

The modern trend, resulting from scientific studies of child life, is away from all "moral" measurements in dealing with babies and young children of the preschool years. This trend has not been brought about because the psychiatrists and students of child life are immoral or because some of them are atheists. Rather they have a more profound faith in human life than the religious heritage has taught men to have. How can one have faith in the Creator of Life if one has lost faith in the real worth of his creation? Dr. Lois Fahs Timmins writes:

A mother who follows the "self-demand" theory of feeding does not think of her baby in terms of "good" or "bad." When the baby cries he is not "bad," but hungry, or tired, or constipated, or lonesome, or sick. When he is quiet he is not "good," but is full, rested, relaxed, and emotionally secure.

When a toddler empties all the bureau drawers it is an expression of need for exploration. When he dumps water all over the bathroom floor it is an expression of need for manipulation. When he hits baby sister it is aggressive behavior expressing jealousy. For doing any of these things the child should not be punished or called "bad," nor should he be praised or called "good" because he refrains from doing them. The solution to these problems lies not in punishment or praise for behavior exhibited, but in meeting the needs expressed by the behavior.[7]

Yet a moralistic attitude toward the behavior of children is almost universally held in our culture. In many church school nurseries, teachers feel conscience stricken if they are not teaching the children to be "kind" and to "share their toys." They tend to give an undue amount of praise for being "good," and too-frequent reproofs for being "selfish." Stories are told to emphasize these virtues: Jesus or God is called upon in prayer to add strength to the children's desire to be "kind."

A director of a city-wide organization of nursery schools (entirely separated from religious institutions) asked her teachers one day to listen carefully to the remarks made by parents on calling for their children at the end of the morning session, and to report at the next teachers' meeting. To their amazement they found that almost uniformly mother after mother asked: "Were you a good boy?" or "Were you a good little girl this morning?" Such unanimity reveals a deep cultural attitude common among adults toward children. From one point of view it deserves appreciation and respect, but from the psychological angle it needs a basic revision. Had these parents been truly imbued with a trust in the children's natural propensities, each would have been eager to discover with what enjoyment and interest her child had spent the morning, knowing full well that if these experiences had been lively, the child's personality would have been growing well.

What has been substituted for the moralistic attitude and ways of dealing with young children is not simply a let-them-do-as-they-please life of chaos. Flexible schedules and certain restraints are still regarded as needed. The little child is not yet able to plan the use of his hours without guidance and suggestion and some control from one who has a larger perspective, and who knows the dangers to be avoided. These controls, however, are made as unobtrusive as is practical, and the child is not made to feel ashamed when he resists. What has been substituted for the moralistic way is a natural, friendly and realistic relationship. Conduct is not dealt with in terms of general rules and principles to be established and obeyed. Instead, situations are faced concretely, better ways are looked for and talked over, or some understanding of the child's special emotional needs leads to a special treatment which will relieve his tensions and his urge to be obstreperous.

Nor does the modern point of view deny the fact that habits of behavior are formed early in a child's life. In fact, human beings are prone to repeat types of behavior that satisfy personal needs and bring satisfaction. It has been found that even when babies have been permitted to decide their own schedules for feeding and sleeping, these schedules have gradually become quite regular if the home life itself is regular. By the time most babies are one year old they have developed certain rather general types of feelings which they express over and over in certain types of action. These emotions and habits of action have usually become so much a part of the child's personality in one year's time that an adult can observe certain basic traits of personality already forming; for example, habits of co-operation or antagonism, aggression or affection, domination or submission, love or hostility, curiosity or withdrawal.

The developmental point of view does not oppose the forming of habits. It does, however, emphasize *the importance of the child's own feelings about his habits*. The external conduct, no matter what it is, is not half so important as whether or not the child finds the action satisfying. Habits are not trained into children merely by forced repetitions of the acts. The child's own feeling of need is primary. Writes Dr. Timmins:

Things done in childhood do not become habits unless the needs the activities satisfy persist beyond childhood. On the contrary, the child of ten who is indecisive is probably the one who was not given sufficient opportunity when two to make up his own mind. The adult who always has to have his own way is the one who was prohibited from having his own way before he was five years old, and so was unable to move on to a more mature level of emotional responses to others. . . . From the developmental point of view, crying is not a habit to be broken by teaching the infant he won't get what he wants by crying, but rather an expression of need which should bring the mother or father promptly to his side to discover the difficulty.[8]

What then is the large and inclusive idea most challenging to religious leaders that becomes clear from this entire discussion of the natural emotional development of the young child? Is it not that *the child's spiritual development begins at the moment of birth? It grows according to a certain schedule of emotional flowering*. These early feeling tones can be changed, but there are natural times for these emotions to be born, to grow and to flower during these early years. All the child's future emotional growth is affected by these beginnings. If these natural and healthy emotions do not come during these years, when nature's schedule has determined they should first come, the child will be emotionally damaged, and the damage may be severe enough to last a lifetime, just as truly as the loss of a leg or of eyesight cannot be made good.

It is as if the child were forming an emotional matrix, in which his religious thinking might be nourished and grow when he is ready to receive from adults the religious ideas they will teach him. If the ideas received fit comfortably within the emotional matrix there is promise of their survival as a real power to vitalize the child's living. His emotions and his thoughts will be able to develop together.

If, however, the ideas do not fit easily within the emotional matrix he has grown, what can he do? Unless he can change his feelings he will resent the imposition of ideas he does not really want. The result will then be a dividing of his personality. He will try to act like a certain kind of person because of some outside influence, yet he will really want secretly to be another kind of person. Or he may twist or remold the ideas, or select only those parts that he can assimilate and try to cast off the rest.

Whether his religion later on will be wholesome and broad in its sympathies will depend, therefore, not only on the reasonableness and clarity of the ideas taught him, but much more on the degree to which he has, in his early childhood, learned to love and to develop a general trust in life. In short, this emotional pattern of personality that has become quite clearly outlined by the end of the first year, and even more clearly defined by the end of the second year, is probably the most significant element that will ever influence his religious growth.

And all this happens when the child is influenced primarily by his parents, before any verbal religious instruction is even possible. It happens before the child is old enough to join a class in any church or school. If parents are left unaware of these new insights, if they are not sensitive to these emotional needs of their children, if they are still bound by the old traditions of discipline and habit training, the whole process of religious development will be weakened at its roots.

4

Natural Beginnings in Children's Curiosities

Each child must plumb vastness and infinity. Let him
call it what he will — fire, water, death God, worlds, stars.
And somehow he must share his curiosity and his awe
before he has too many static answers. . . . — We forget
that the probing of strange phenomena, creation, God,
death, magic, has made our scientists, our artists, our
religious leaders, throughout the ages. Why should we
shorten this probing or cover it up for children?
— C. MADELEINE DIXON

WE HAVE CONSIDERED how confidently we can rely on the
newborn child's impulsive hunger for love as the first step in
a natural spiritual development. We have also considered how
a young child grows emotionally, in his power to love, trust
and co-operate. We have spoken of the compulsion to grow
according to a certain sequence of steps. Now let us look at
a young child's curiosity or urge to learn the truth — another
value which all high religions have cherished. This urge becomes clearly apparent when young children have learned
to talk well enough to ask questions about things. This active
period of questioning usually appears between the ages of
three and four, and may last with growing intensity for three
or more years.

Dr. Werner Wolff, in his remarkable book entitled *The Personality of the Preschool Child: His Search for His Self,* makes
an impressive point. As a result of his extensive observations
of young children, he has come to the conclusion that "the
young child does not explore the world only in order to gain
knowledge": "All expressions of personality by the young

47

child seemed to be variations on one theme, the child's search for his self. The imagery, his spoken language, and the language of his behavior appear as the continuous questioning: Who am I? What am I for? The child's search for his origin is the most important part of his inquiry about the world he lives in. The question whence he came and how he was made is linked up with his questions about the structure and origin of everything."[1]

Dr. Wolff says that "if the adult were to start asking 'why' about everything in his life he would be unable to live. The adult, therefore, limits his questioning only to problems which are essential to his personality." The child whose orbit of experience is still limited has not learned to restrict his curiosities. His "thought is thus continuously troubled, because he is in a state of continuous search for his self."[2]

Dr. Arnold Gesell and his associates, who have observed hundreds of preschool children, report that the questions come usually in this order — where, what, why, who and how, representing, it would seem, a deeper and deeper plumbing on the part of the child to find a kind of wholeness of meaning.[3] This reaching out for more and more understanding is sometimes so intense that the young child becomes a runabout question mark. With growth in the use of language and with widening social contacts and with more experiences in the ever-present world of nature, the young child tries slowly to weave a philosophic web by which to cling securely to life.

Those of us who have been privileged to be associated with young children in our homes and in schools of religion where the young are encouraged to express their yearnings freely, have often been amazed at the far-reaching implications of the questions even such small children ask. A Vassar student followed a four-year-old boy about the nursery for a couple of weeks, listening to what he said and noting down his questions. Among the many questions she reported are the following:

"How thick is the sky? Is it different from the ground?"

"Does it hurt the ground to have holes in it?"

"Why are shadows there? Why are they crooked? When will they go away?"

"Where does light come from?"

"How does the clock know what time it is?"

"When am I not a little boy and am a big man?"

"Why is it when you have a birthday you are older?"

"What house was I in before I was born? I couldn't see then because I was inside my mother's tummy. I couldn't see or hear anything when I was inside my mummy."

"What is my back like? You can't see your own face, can you?"

"How do you see? If you are blind how do you not see?"

"Don't you think it's funny about people's blood being inside their skin? Is my insides a pipe?"

"When I am asleep I have dreams and I see things. But how can I?"

"My eyes are shut if I'm asleep, aren't they? But how can I see things in dreams unless my eyes are open?"

"A voice is a fast thing, isn't it? Where is your voice?"

"Is it in your mouth? Are all the words stored up in your mouth?"

"Why do I have two eyes when I can see with one? It would be better to have one of them in the back, wouldn't it?"

"What does it feel like to be a worm?"

"What does a little stick of wood feel?"

"How does it feel to die?"

An unusual child! Brilliant and imaginative! Yes, but in this exceptional child do we not have a sign of the potential wonderings of every young child? This boy's sensitive feelings were reaching out this way and that in an effort to know and identify himself with everything he touched. He was wondering about the mystery of the passing of time, and the mystery of sound and speech. He was wondering about his own birth, about death, about his power to dream. He was curious about his own body, inside and out, and about the things he could do and could not do. He wanted to feel with the blind and with the dead, and even with sticks and stones.

Apparently he felt secure in the affection and understanding of his parents, but life was already much larger than his parents' arms could contain. He was feeling out for a security in a wider world, where he was realizing that he had, in a sense, to face life alone. This larger security is what religious beliefs sometimes bring to young children. The very way children probe for understanding is evidence of the importance to them of some kind of over-all point of view.

This urge to understand what life is all about is expressed not only in a young child's questioning, but also in his play. For adults, play is recreation, a way of escaping from the seriousness or the routines of living. But for the young child, his play is a way of experimenting with life, of digging deeper and exploring more widely into its meaning. A child's toys are his library, and his nursery and playground are his laboratories. His play is serious business — enjoyable, yes, but all-absorbing and filled with meaning. In his play the child tries to learn how it feels to be somebody else, or he sets himself the task of reliving parts of his own experiences in order to know himself and others better.

If then this interpretation of what children are really after in their early questioning is correct, we need not feel a need to hurry them faster than they naturally wish to go. Even though most of their queries may seem far removed from what adults call religion, yet we will realize that each small bit of understanding gained will become a part of the child's philosophy of life when he feels the need consciously to put everything together. Surely, when a child asks for so much to feed his thinking in the immediate present, we should not rush to give him words beyond his understanding which we think he will wish to know someday in the future. Why try to pull a child up to the top rung of the ladder when on his own he can stretch only to the lowest rung? The very nature of the child's own growth seems to assure us that in religion as well as in every other phase of living we can trust the child's natural schedule of development.

A few years ago some of us felt keenly the need to experiment with a more natural way of religious education by starting with children's own experiences, and then moving along with them according to the natural sequence of their own growing. We therefore gathered from our records of young children's activities as many reports as we could of their philosophic questionings. We studied these to find out what types of occasions provoked the deeper and more far-reaching wonderings, and the kinds of matters about which the children raised their questions.

With this direct observation of young children we began to study also the more recent books written by anthropologists and students of early forms of religion. We wanted to find out how religious beliefs and practices began in the history of the human race. Did religious faith arise full-orbed as a result of some special revelation to the first man? Or did mankind in his racial childhood build up his religion naturally out of his own experiences with life? We tried to discover what kinds of experiences had challenged him most strongly, and had required of him the development of a religious philosophy and of religious ceremonies. The results of this inquiry into the history of religion yielded certain unforgettable impressions, and increased our respect for the child-people of the race who lived before the printed word.

Our study made clear that man became religious because of the very nature of his world, and because of his own needs. Before he had learned to make arrows, or to cultivate the soil, primitive man felt his world alive with power. He felt invisible and living powers in the wind and rain, in thunder and lightning, and he sought ways of control and protection. He felt an invisible life in things both large and small — in animals, trees, fire, water. He was awed by the rising and setting of the sun, and was both comforted and frightened by the waxing and waning of the moon. Primitive man felt such a close kinship with animals that he learned to ask their forgiveness for killing them or eating their flesh.

Primitive man was sensitive to the Mystery of life. He felt it whenever he witnessed the birth of animals, or saw his own newborn offspring. When that unknown caveman first molded an image of divinity in the form of a pregnant woman he was expressing his feeling for the wonder of creation. And when Neanderthal man first buried his dead and laid beside the motionless corpse a chain of beads or a stone knife, he was expressing his feeling that death did not destroy all. In his sleep he had recognized that something invisible within him could transcend the body; so in death he saw a similar possibility. The world of spirit was very real to primitive man. He felt himself immersed in mystery, and he set out to try to penetrate it.

In spite of all the superstitious content of his thought, it must be admitted that it was the savage who created religion, and not civilized man. The untutored cave-dwelling man, who could neither read nor count, nor even perhaps converse with coherence, was the one who began "the biggest experiment that mankind has ever attempted."[4] He began to feel his way into a philosophy of life which would keep his heart warm in spite of all the terrors he experienced. Primitive man began to experiment to find out not only the nature of the world he could see, but also the nature of the invisible forces he could not see. In short, mankind's religious beliefs and practices grew naturally out of his experiences with life and because of his own inner emotional needs.

And what of the results of our study of the experiences of small children today? Our interest grew as we gathered the records, for we discovered a remarkable parallel between the kinds of experiences which had aroused primitive man and the kinds which occasioned young children's questionings. We found that children under five, even in our protective culture, had to face the three major mysteries of existence, birth, sex, and death, and that they were fascinated and awed by their contacts. We learned also that young children feel the threat and overpowering greatness of the large forces of nature — the wind, rain, storm, and thunder — and often find real difficulty in adjusting their personal desires to these realities. We found that even during this preschool period, children usually become aware of their dreaming, and sense the privacy of their own real invisibility. We found also that feelings of great excitement and sometimes of distress came with their first awareness of great spaces and of the movement of the earth. We found them awed by awakening feelings for the passing of time. Some wept with their first realization that once they were not existing, and that sometime they might be living when their parents would be dead.

In short, we realized, as a result of our observations, that life long ago and life today are basically the same. We became confident that there are elements in the very nature of our world and of ourselves that challenge even young children to yearn for a larger and more understanding security than their parents or even our scientific civilization can supply. We became convinced that as a result of the very nature of life, small children have emotional experiences that are the seeds of religious sentiment; and that the natural way of spiritual guidance would begin with these experiences and let the larger understandings grow slowly as the experiences increased.

When, therefore, we were given the opportunity to prepare stories for use by preschool children which might help to encourage this natural process of religious development, we had a basis for selecting the types of experiences to portray.[5] We were not interested simply in entertaining children. Nor did we care to write stories to teach them to obey the great commandments, or to present moral principles for them to follow. We felt no need to teach such young children to be kind or honest, or to tell them about God. Nor did we think it necessary to tell them stories from the Bible in order to have a book of religiously significant stories. The choices for the episodes grew out of the study we had made of the kinds of experiences that had been found to be especially provocative of wonder and thought, both in the experience of the race, and also in the daily experiences of the young children of this generation whom we had observed. The stories we wrote deal with the following kinds of experiences.[6]

1. Experiences are told in which the two story-children, Martin and Judy, face the great forces or universal phenomena of nature, such as the wind, the rain, the snow, the sun and moon.

2. Experiences are related in which the contrast between animate and inanimate things becomes apparent. When a child becomes aware that a living baby or animal can feel and move and grow, and that a doll or Teddy bear cannot do so, he is brought face to face with the mystery of being alive.

3. Experiences with birth, such as seeing newborn kittens, the hatching of chickens, or watching a newborn baby, dramatize the mystery of life. Anything of deep significance in a child's religion is dependent on this discovery of the wonder of life.

4. Experiences with death are also included for a child's first close experience with death is necessarily a challenge. To discover that one's own life has a beginning and an end brings perspective to one's outlook. A young child can sense but a small measure of the meaning of death, but knowing death comes early.

5. Experiences with pain and sickness are often crucial in

a child's spiritual growth. Sickness sometimes leads to increased respect for the body, and to the learning of patience under painful and trying circumstances. On the other hand, sickness sometimes leads to the growth of fear of unseen dangers, to feelings of undue dependence and helplessness. Some high values and some unwholesome trends are latent as possibilities in children's early experiences with sickness.

6. Some of the narratives present the children playing with their shadows. Young children are universally fascinated and sometimes made afraid by their shadows. If there is fear, they need to be relieved of it, and lead to understanding and enjoyment of their shadows.

7. The child becomes conscious of dreaming during these early years. The distinction between the world of reality (as we frequently call it) and the world of fancy is not easy for him to make. When he begins to sense the difference he is better able to cope with his fears. It must be a time of awakening when a child is first aware that his thoughts can travel unseen, and that in fancy he can go beyond the boundaries marked by his hands and feet, or his ears and eyes. There is something thrilling in the thought that our greatest powers are invisible — our power to think, to imagine, and to feel. How can a child really catch the significance of the invisibility of God until he has first realized the invisibility of his own psyche?

8. A number of the stories were written to portray the child's feelings of social relatedness to others, sometimes within the family circle, sometimes in the larger community beyond the home. These are germinal experiences from which the larger feelings of human brotherhood grow.

9. Then there are experiences of an opposite sort that bring feelings of isolation, hostility, rejection. In these the child is challenged to look for the reasons for these undesirable conditions and to study cause and effect in social relations. Through these experiences he may learn to identify his own

feelings with those of others, and so begin to feel sympathy.

10. There are stories portraying certain personal achievements — the creation of something new and valuable, the doing of something original, or the overcoming of some difficulty. Such experiences are a tonic to the spirit.

11. Experiences are narrated in which choices have to be made. Sometimes a present good is compared with a future postponed good. Sometimes the choice made leads to unhappiness. Learning by one's mistakes is often even more fruitful than learning by one's successes.

12. Finally, in the volume written for five- and six-year-olds, Martin and Judy, the two story-children, are found puzzling over thoughts of God, and taking their first steps in prayer. Such thinking of God is brought about by the children's own wonderings, and praying is presented in a way that can have some meaning for the young child.

13. There are also several stories telling of the celebrations of religious ceremonials. In these stories, only those features are presented which can be understood by young children. The feelings that can be shared by all are accented.

Our purpose in preparing these stories was to accent certain significant experiences in a child's natural religious growth by putting them into the stories of two imaginary children. If the children who hear these stories can identify their own feelings with those of Martin and Judy, the significance of their own experiences may be increased for them. The kinds of experiences narrated are not the kind that can always be easily talked over. In many homes parents feel tongue-tied. They can answer their children's questions only in traditional phrases. Sometimes, however, these primary experiences stir children deeply. If their questions are not treated with understanding and full respect, the children may be left with feelings of guilt.

There is also a volume written especially for the parents, entitled *Consider the Children: How They Grow*.[7] In it the philosophy of a natural, developmental way of spiritual guidance of children of preschool age is set forth more fully than it is possible to do in this present volume, whose scope includes children of all ages.

This natural way of encouraging a child's spiritual growth through accenting and dwelling on his own significant experiences is, we believe, based on the findings of psychology and of history, as well as on experimental work with young children. This philosophy is based also on the conviction that vital religion must in large measure be a personal creation rather than primarily the gift of society to the child, or a body of beliefs accepted because authoritatively revealed.

A minister, who had long held the idea that a young child's first introduction to religion should be by means of simply told Bible stories, finally adopted an experimental attitude. He read the Martin and Judy stories to his five-year-old daughter. Night after night for months she asked for them. Finally, when the father had the opportunity to make a confession to the authors, he did so, saying: "You and Anne have finally converted me. You could not have done it alone. As I have been observing what those stories have done for Anne I have changed my point of view. I am sure now that she has gotten more real spiritual help from hearing those Martin and Judy stories than she could ever have received from hearing Bible stories."

When children become older, the heritage from the past and the rituals and ceremonies that live in the society to which the children belong will inevitably influence them. As their social horizons broaden, they will become curious to learn why people do things as they do. They will be led naturally into the past to find out who were the first people to pray and why. They will wish to examine the Bible records. First of all, however, children need to have many opportunities to learn and notice for themselves. With sensitive and understanding adults as their companions and counselors, they need their own firsthand, direct relations with the universe. They need to discover that "people have learned all of what we know about God by seeing for themselves what is in his world." They need to notice for themselves "what belongs to God" before someone has told them.

Because an understanding of the religious heritage from the past is important for the older child, we shall examine in the two following chapters our Judeo-Christian heritage as it has been embodied in "the Bible." What are the old treasures there which the oncoming generation should know and appreciate? How may we help young people to become wise householders who can choose between the treasures and the useless antiques, and so find themselves blessed by both what is old and what is new?

5

The Old Bible: The Story of Salvation

> Our fathers had their religion. . . . It saved them, it
> built character, it made life serious, it was an heroic creed
> which has lost credence in our more knowing and more
> frivolous age.
>
> — JOHN BURROUGHS

NO PROBLEM IN THE RELIGIOUS EDUCATION of children in our
Western culture is so omnipresent as this one: What shall we
do about the Bible? The large and continuous sales of juvenile Bible-story books is evidence of the importance of the
Bible for children in the minds of parents and teachers. Those
books that preserve the actual words of the Bible have an
especially strong appeal regardless of whether or not the children hearing or reading the stories can understand the language. There seems to be a vague popular expectation that
Bible stories will be good for children, and that the earlier
they become acquainted with even the names of the Bible
characters the better.

Furthermore, in most churches of the West, a children's
school of religion is regarded generally as a Bible school.
Bible stories pre-empt the time schedules in most Sunday
schools of Christendom, and the Biblical history and literature
of the Hebrew people as recorded in the Old Testament com-
prise the main subject matter in most Jewish synagogue
schools.

In spite of this common and long-time emphasis on the
Bible in the religious homes and schools of our country, the

59

fact remains that as an adult generation we are woefully ignorant of the contents of the Bible, and that the younger generation is still more ignorant of it. Nor does this ignorance prevail merely among the non-churched masses of children; it is also prevalent in only a slightly less degree among children who have faithfully attended religious schools throughout their childhood. A number of studies have been made which point out the truth of these statements.

A professor in a college located in the so-called Bible belt recently gave his students a test on their Biblical knowledge. To his dismay he discovered that although a majority of his students had attended Sunday school regularly throughout childhood, most of them were grossly ill-informed and confused. When he was discussing the results with his class, one of them burst out with this resentful remark: "It makes me mad as fire when I think of the time I spent going to Sunday school and then realize how ignorant I am of the Bible and my own religion."

Being aroused and challenged by what he had learned, the professor determined to find out, if he could, why an intelligent young woman could attend Sunday school and young people's meetings for fifteen years and be left so ignorant of the literary heritage of her church. So he examined all the Sunday school literature that was being used in the local church of his denomination. He studied the materials used by teachers whose classes ranged in age from six to the early twenties.

His conclusion was that a student could have read everything available, and still be left with the vague and confused ideas regarding the characters and events portrayed in the Bible which his college students had revealed in the tests he gave them. He writes: "The dominant tone of much of this material . . . is argument rather than education, propaganda rather than teaching; all with the assumption of absolute truth. . . . Verses extracted from the various Gospels serve to flavor sure-fire panaceas for all the ills of our complicated industrial system. Or they provide a one-shot cure for the international maladies of a sick world."[1]

Although this illustration may present an extreme example of the inadequacy of the Biblical teaching being done in church and synagogue schools, yet the ignorance shown by it is too prevalent to be taken lightly.

What is the trouble? Why is there on the one hand this strong pressure from the general public to have the Bible taught to children and young people, while at the same time the younger generation has been left in truth so ignorant? Is the popular demand merely the remnant of a traditional and unexamined attitude toward the Bible? Do the churches and synagogues really wish their children to read the Bible intelligently? Or are our religious leaders more concerned to preserve "the faith" than to have their children become intelligent regarding their literary heritage?

These questions lead to further ones. Why should children and young people know the Bible? How relevant are these ancient records to the problems of today's world? Will knowing the Bible tend to make children better fitted to help create the new kind of society that our world so sorely needs?

If we are to answer these questions intelligently we must ask a prior question: What kind of a book are people talking about when they say "the Bible"? Is it the Bible as our ancestors interpreted it and as it is still interpreted by orthodox groups? Or is it the Bible that modern Biblical scholarship and the new knowledge of the history of religion have brought to light?

The difference between these two concepts of the Bible is so great that one can appropriately say they represent two different books, an old and a new Bible. Almost everything that is really important in the message of the old Bible of orthodox Christianity and Judaism is changed when one reads the new Bible as interpreted by modern Biblical scholars and students of history. To discover how basic the difference is between these two Bibles let us examine each in some detail. It is possible that we may discover from such an examination one reason why so much Bible teaching is ineffectual.

The old Bible of Christian and Jewish orthodoxy is looked upon as the true revelation of God's purpose on behalf of humanity. Beginning with the creation of the world and ending with the creation of a new heaven and a new earth, it is one continued story from Genesis through Revelation. God's actions are the ones that produce the dramatic crises. The main character is God himself. Although the books in this Bible were actually written by different authors and in different periods, yet this old Bible is regarded as one consistent story. The God who spoke in the Garden of Eden, the God of Abraham, Isaac and Jacob, the God of Mt. Sinai, the God of Isaiah and of Malachi, the God of Jesus and of Paul — all of these are assumed to be one and the same God, the only true God of all the earth.

As the Christian church has understood this old Bible, it is the record of God's divine plan for mankind's destiny — it is "The Great Story of Salvation." This is not thought of as a great myth. It is a divinely inspired record of the history of man. This Bible story is based on what are believed to be actual happenings and also on what are described as direct revelations from God of the meanings of those happenings and on divine revelations of what the future holds in store. The old Story of the Bible begins in eternity and closes in eternity.

For orthodox Jews the Old Testament portion of this old Bible, with the addition of several other important books not included in the Christian canon, has been their sacred book. The Hebrews, therefore, were the originators of the general pattern of this Story of the Bible. In orthodox terms we would say the Hebrews were the first to receive the divine revelation. The stories in both the Christian and the Jewish Bibles, up to the birth of Jesus, have the same general pattern. The

Hebrew sacred book, however, is an unfinished revelation with the person of the Messiah or world Savior left unknown, although his coming was promised. The Jewish Bible, like the Christian Bible, contains the promise of a final Judgment Day and the establishment of a Kingdom of Righteousness, with the punishment or destruction of all evil-doers.

Let us then review this Story of the Bible as orthodox Christianity has interpreted it. Since St. Augustine of the fifth century was one of the earliest of the church fathers to put into writing the Christian interpretation of God's dealings with Israel, and since his form of the Story of Salvation has been the most influential during these fifteen hundred years, we shall follow his outline. In his time the number seven was regarded as a sacred number; it was natural, therefore, that when he wrote the outline of this great drama he should conceive of it as happening in seven great ages of time.[2]

The First Great Age of Time

In the beginning was God. "The earth was without form, and void; and darkness was upon the face of the deep."

"And the spirit of God moved upon the face of the waters." He spoke. The earth, the sun, moon and stars were created. He spoke again; and all kinds of plants and trees, all kinds of animals, insects, fishes and birds were also created. Last of all he created the first man and woman, forming them in his own image. He breathed into them the breath of life. He endowed them with immortality, and placed them in a beautiful and fertile garden, where they were to live at ease and multiply, and fill the earth with their descendants. To this first blessed couple God gave every privilege but one. He commanded them to refrain from eating the fruit of one tree in the garden — the Tree of the Knowledge of Good and Evil.

In heaven the immortal angels had always obeyed God implicitly, until one named Satan stirred up a rebellion. Because of his disobedience he had been cast out of heaven and was now allowed to wander upon the newly created earth. Having learned of the restriction which God had made on the liberties of the first man and woman, Satan saw his opportunity for revenge. Changing his shape into that of a talking snake, he tempted Eve, and Adam through Eve, to eat the forbidden fruit, assuring them that it would be very desirable to know good from evil, and that no real harm would come to them.

The first woman and man yielded to this temptation. As a consequence, God drove them out of the beautiful garden, to live where it became necessary for them to work and sweat for their food. To the woman, who had been the first to yield, and to all her female descendants God added two special punishments: childbirth would be painful, and woman would forever hold a position of inferiority in relation to man. For both Adam and Eve and for all their descendants two final punishments were added. Immortality was taken from them, and thus death entered the world. By the process of inheritance, all human beings from then on have been born with two opposing natures, one good and one evil. That day, therefore, when Adam and Eve consciously sinned, was the most momentous day in all human history.

Thus the First Great Age of Time ended in tragedy and disaster.

The Second Great Age of Time

Years passed. Children and grandchildren were born. As one generation lived and died, another was born to take its place. With each new generation, quarreling, hatred, murder increased. Finally God, looking down from heaven and seeing that man's thoughts were continually evil, repented that he had ever created man. In his great disappointment God resolved to remove from the face of the earth not only mankind but beasts, birds and creeping things of all kinds.

Finding one righteous man, however, God altered his intentions, and decided to save Noah and his family and one male and female of every kind of living thing. He commanded Noah to build an ark large enough to contain all these creatures. Then follows the well-known story of Noah's ark, of the world-wide flood, of the fresh beginning after the flood, and of God's rainbow promise never to repeat this punishment.

God then blessed Noah and his family and said to them, "Be fruitful and populate the earth."

Once more the children of men multiplied. Some became farmers, and planted vineyards and made wine from the grapes. Soon even Noah himself was drinking to excess. One day his son Ham found his father lying in his tent completely drunk and naked, and reported the fact to his two brothers. When Noah regained his senses, he was so angry with Ham for what he had done that he cursed him and his descendants, condemning them to unending slavery. But he blessed the descendants of Shem and Japheth.

Some of Noah's descendants wandered eastward and found a fertile plain where they settled and learned to build houses of brick. Since at that time they all spoke one language, they were able to work together and to accomplish great things. Some even learned to build high towers. They dreamed that someday they would be able to reach even up to heaven, the dwelling place of God. But God was displeased with man's overweening pride, and said to himself: "There will be no end to what man will try to do unless I stop him in some way."

So God came down to earth and by his great power he confused man's speech, and caused each one to talk in a language unknown to anyone else. Being unable, therefore, to understand one another, the people had to abandon their great building projects. Then God forced these confused sons of men to scatter far and wide over the earth. Because of what God did that day, the tower that was begun and never finished was called the tower of Babel, meaning Confusion, and ever since that time the peoples of the earth have spoken many different languages.

Thus the Second Great Age of Time ended in confusion.

The Third Great Age of Time

Many years went by. In spite of warnings and punishments from God, the people of the earth continued to follow the selfish desires of their own hearts. God, seeing their great wickedness and knowing that their very natures had been defiled by the disobedience of Adam and Eve, realized that he could no longer hope to save all mankind. He must try a new plan.

Once more God searched the earth to find a righteous man after his own heart. At last he chose Abraham, a rich shepherd living on the outskirts of the wicked city of Ur beside the Euphrates River.

Appearing to Abraham in a dream, God said: "Go out from this idol-worshiping people, leave your relatives and your father's house, and go forth into another land which I will show you. There I will prosper you if you and your descendants will obey my voice. Your name shall become great among the nations and you shall be a blessing to all mankind."

Abraham arose in obedience to God. With his father Terah and his own family and servants and flocks he journeyed toward the land of Canaan. Wherever they pitched their tents, whether under some great oak or beside a bubbling spring or on a hilltop, Abraham always built an altar and made a sacrifice to God.

God, therefore, prospered Abraham and his tribe. They grew rapidly in numbers and in riches; they either conquered or made friends with the people already in the land of Canaan. But the inhabitants of Canaan were wicked, and a temptation to Abraham's people. To show his disapproval of their wickedness, God destroyed two of the worst Canaanite cities, Sodom and Gomorrah, by raining down fire and brimstone upon them. Abraham's nephew barely escaped with his life.

The years came and went. Abraham's grandson Jacob wrestled one night with an angel of God, and won. He was therefore granted God's special blessing and given the new name Israel, meaning "one who has prevailed with God."

Now Israel had twelve sons and they were unable to live in peace together, for eleven of them were jealous of Joseph, the one brother who had become their father's favorite. Secretly they plotted his ruin; and when the occasion offered they sold him to a gang of Midianites who were on their way to Egypt. There Joseph was resold and became a slave in Pharaoh's household.

But God was with Joseph and helped him to become a favorite with the keeper of the prison. Before long Joseph was in charge of all the other prisoners. Indeed he grew so rapidly in wisdom and in favor with those about him that he was before long freed from prison and promoted from one office to another, until he was given a position of national power next to the Pharaoh.

In the meantime, the people in the land of Canaan were suffering from a severe famine. Israel and his family were reduced to such great want that several of the sons traveled down into Egypt to buy food.

Their surprise and shame were beyond speaking when these brothers discovered that the man in the palace before whom they had to make their plea for grain was none other than their brother Joseph. But Joseph spoke kindly to his brothers and told them not to be angry with themselves, for God had been guiding them all along. "Hasten back to Father," said Joseph, "and bring him down here with all of the family."

So the sons of Israel and their families sojourned in Egypt for many years. During that time they increased in numbers and in possessions, and as long as Jacob and Joseph lived God gave them peace. Thus the years passed contentedly until there arose a Pharaoh in Egypt who had never heard of Joseph. He said: "There are too many Hebrews here. If our country should have to go to war, these foreigners might take up arms against us."

This new Pharaoh forced the Hebrews to labor as his slaves. He required them to make bricks and to build great buildings. He put over them taskmasters who treated them cruelly.

Finally the children of Israel in their bitter plight cried unto God for a deliverer to save them from their great oppression and disgrace. But God withheld his help from his "Chosen People" for a time. They needed the lesson of longer suffering if they were to learn how to live obediently and righteously before him.

Thus, the Third Great Age of Time ended in sorrow and crying.

The Fourth Great Age of Time

Finally in his great goodness, God brought his "Chosen People" another deliverer. This time it was a Hebrew who had been adopted into Pharaoh's household when a baby, and who had all through his life been treated as a royal son. At God's command, Moses left the luxury of Pharaoh's court and risked his life in order to free his people. With God's help he performed one miracle after another, until the Pharaoh was so frightened that he consented to let the Hebrew slaves go free, commanding them to leave the country.

In order that they might escape before Pharaoh changed his mind, God enabled Moses to divide the waters of the Red Sea so that his people could cross on dry land. As they moved on eastward across the desert of Arabia toward the land of Canaan, God continually directed and protected them, and miraculously supplied food for them when it was needed.

God made a covenant with Moses and his people. If they would obey his commands and worship him only, God would continue to bless them. He would lead them back into the land of Canaan. They would be his "Chosen People," and he would be their chosen God. With his power to help them they would be able to conquer the whole country and would in time become a very great nation. God even wrote with his own hand on two tablets of stone his ten most important commandments so that all would know what was right and what was wrong.

Alas! In spite of all God's special help to his "Chosen People," and in spite of all the great wonders and miraculous signs that he had performed to save them from their dreary slavery in Egypt, the people of Israel did not fulfill their part of the covenant with God. Some made a golden image of a calf and worshiped it instead of the true God. Others complained of their hardships in the desert and wished they were back in Egypt. Even Moses grew discouraged and fell short of God's expectations. Because his people had forsaken him, God punished them all by requiring them to wander aimlessly through the desert for forty years. Even Moses himself died before his people were allowed to enter the "Promised Land." For hundreds of years there arose no prophet in Israel like Moses, one whom "God knew face to face."

So the Fourth Great Age of Time ended, as had the other ages before it, in sore disappointment.

The Fifth Great Age of Time

God was still long-suffering and forgiving and would not forsake his people forever. He raised up another brave leader, a daring fighter named Joshua, to take Moses' place. God did great wonders for Joshua also. He divided the waters of the Jordan so that his people could walk across quickly on the dry river bed. He caused the walls of the great city of Jericho to come tumbling down at a trumpeter's signal so that his people could burn the city and destroy all its inhabitants. From there this invading band went from town to town, up and down the country. When they disobeyed God's commands they met defeat in battle. When they obeyed and remained loyal to Jehovah they were given the victory.

At last a large section of Canaan was conquered, and God allowed his people to have a king. As a result their prestige with their neighbors grew. King Saul was succeeded by an even greater leader. King David conquered the great citadel of Jerusalem and made it the country's capital. He extended the boundaries of the kingdom beyond the Jordan.

After David came King Solomon, to whom God gave not only the greatest wisdom, but also enormous wealth and a long life. Solomon's ships sailed across the Mediterranean as well as down the Red Sea to trade in Africa and even in India. King Solomon employed thousands of workmen. Some cut down cedars in Lebanon; others dug copper from the rocky cliffs of Edom; others smelted the copper in mines that Solomon had built. Thousands of craftsmen worked continually for him in gold, silver and copper, creating beautiful vessels for the royal palaces, while other thousands of skilled workers embroidered linen and silken apparel and curtains. The appointments in his own palace, his throne and his eating vessels were beyond compare. As his crowning achievement King Solomon built the magnificent temple in Jerusalem to the glory of Jehovah, and established the elaborate rituals of worship appropriate in this impressive place. During King Solomon's reign the glory of Israel reached its greatest height.

Alas! With their growing luxury and wealth the people of Israel became proud and degenerate. They turned from the God of righteousness and began to worship the gods of the Canaanites and of the other nations around them. They did that which was evil in the sight of God as did the other nations around them. The great Kingdom of Solomon was divided into two kingdoms. For every king who did that which was good in the sight of the Lord his God there were two or more who worshiped foreign gods and "provoked to anger the

Lord God of Israel." God sent Elijah, Elisha, Amos, Isaiah, Jeremiah, and others, one after the other, but the people would not heed their warnings. God punished his people with famines and pestilences, and again and again allowed some neighboring nation to invade the land, conquering some portion or requiring heavy tribute. But king after king did that which was evil in the sight of God and made his people to sin. Only rarely did a good king rule. For three and a half centuries and more the two little nations grew steadily weaker. Finally, God allowed first the northern and then the southern capital cities to be captured. Thousands of the people were killed, and other thousands were led into captivity in Babylon.

For over half a millennium the further story of this people is a story of wars and conquest by one great power after another. The people of God became a people of great sorrow, knowing both suffering and grief — yet ever praying and longing for deliverance. One great hope soothed their pain. They believed that someday God would send them a divine deliverer who would be able to defeat all their enemies and who would set up a world-wide kingdom of righteousness with Jerusalem as the capital city. They believed that a God-chosen descendant of their first great King David would reign for ever and ever over a world at peace. But the waiting was long and filled with bitter grief.

So the Fifth Great Age of Time ended in near-despair.

The Sixth Great Age of Time

Surely the people of the earth, including even the "Chosen People," deserved to be destroyed. Their sinfulness had grown to such proportions that only God alone could save them. They could not turn and be saved in their own strength. Yet God's righteousness must be revealed. He must in some way show his righteous anger. Someone must be punished. Someone's life must be given as a ransom for the sins of all the world. The goodness of this one life must be equal in power to all the evil of all the world. Only a divine sacrifice would be equal to such a great need. There was but one such person — God's only begotten Son. Was God willing to have his Son's life sacrificed for the sake of the world's sinners? This was the great question, but God had foreseen that the decision would have to be made, and he was prepared. God's love for mankind was boundless.

So it came to pass that in his great mercy God sent his only begotten Son from heaven to earth to become a substitute sacrifice for the sins of all humanity. Born miraculously in the womb of a virgin, the Son of God became a little child who was named Jesus. The glory of his birth was sung by angels from heaven. He to whom the earth and sky belonged labored at a carpenter's bench. He went about preaching the Word of God. By merely a command he made the sick well, the lame walk, the blind see. By the word of his mouth he even brought the dead back to life.

But the "Chosen People" refused to accept their divine deliverer. They made charges of conspiracy against him. They brought him to be tried before Pilate. They pressed for his condemnation. They mocked his assertion that he was their Messiah. They rejected the evidence of his miracles. They placed a crown of thorns on his head and laughed at his claim to be a king. Finally, Jesus the Savior was killed as a common criminal in the tortures of crucifixion.

God's "Beloved Son" could have avoided this death. He could have prayed God to send his angels down from heaven to save him from this great suffering, but he gave up his life willingly, in order that God's righteousness might be vindicated. The death of the divine Son was the ransom that had to be paid for the sins of the world, and Jesus Christ was "obedient unto death."

But death could not hold the Son of God. On the third morning after his burial angels came down from heaven, rolled away the stone from the door of the tomb and entered it. Then the Son of God rose from his grave and walked again on the earth, to the amazement of all who saw him. For forty days, now here and now there, the Son of God was seen by his former friends and disciples.

This was the final sign needed to show that God had accepted his Son's great sacrifice as a wholly adequate atonement. Thus Jesus, the Son of God, became the Savior of the world. Whosoever confesses his sin and believes in this Savior is thereby saved from the eternal punishment his sins deserve, and shall have everlasting life.

Jesus' farewell came when he was with his disciples on the top of a mountain. He had given them his final command: "Go ye into all the world and preach the gospel to the whole creation. Lo, I am with you always, even unto the end of the world."[3] When Jesus had finished speaking he was lifted up slowly from the earth higher and higher until he disappeared from sight, to be welcomed by his Father in heaven.

So the Sixth Great Age of Time came to its glorious end.

The Seventh Great Age of Time

For days the disciples were stunned, both by their grief and by their wondrous joy. They had seen a great miracle. They believed that this Jesus, their friend, with whom they used to eat and sleep and talk, was really the Son of God, the Messiah for whom their people had been longing: and yet — he had not saved Israel. His whole life and teachings had been discredited. He had been held up to scorn before all the people of Jerusalem as a conspirator and criminal. But he had risen from the dead! He had ascended into heaven! And he was going to return to the earth in glory and power! Everyone would recognize him as the Messiah then.

As the disciples were meeting together in an upper room, talking over their memories of things that used to happen when Jesus was with them, another amazing thing occurred. They began to grow restless, afire with a zeal to leave their homes and go from town to town telling the wonderful story as Jesus had commanded them to do. To their surprise it seemed as though a little flame rested on each man's head.

In their excitement they began talking, and to their surprise they found themselves talking in different languages. This was the final proof that they should go into other countries outside Palestine, yes, into "all the world," for now they could tell the wondrous story in whatever language was spoken.

These, then, were the first missionaries of the gospel. They went forth in the assurance that Christ would soon return to the earth in glory, to rule the whole world in peace and righteousness. Although Jesus did not return during their lifetime, and although he has not returned to this day, the promise of his second coming still holds. When this Christ does come he shall be the King of all kings and Lord of all lords, and he shall reign on the earth for a thousand years. Then righteousness and peace shall cover the earth as the waters cover the sea.

At last the final great Day of Judgment shall come. God and his Son shall sit upon a white throne. All the dead shall be raised. All people great and small, the living and those who have died, shall stand before the throne of God, and the Son of God shall judge each one according to his deeds upon the earth. Then the Book of Life shall be opened, in which are written the names of all those who have been accepted by God. Those whose names have been written in this book shall be ushered into heaven; and the first heaven and the first earth shall pass away. In this new heaven "there shall be no more death, neither sorrow, nor crying, neither shall there be any more pain."[4] "But there shall in no wise enter into it anything that defileth, neither whatsoever worketh abomination, or maketh a lie; but they which are written in the Lamb's book of life."[5]

And a great chorus shall rise in heaven singing: "Alleluia!

Salvation and glory and honour and power unto the lord our God: for true and righteous are his judgments."[6] And the voices of this multitude shall sound like "the voice of many waters, and as the voice of mighty thunderings, saying Alleluia, for the Lord God omnipotent reigneth. Let us be glad and rejoice, and give honour to him."[7]

All sinners — those whose names are not in the Book of Life — shall be cast with Satan into the lake of fire and brimstone, "where they shall be tormented day and night for ever and ever."[8]

So the Seventh Great Age of Time shall come to an end and eternity shall begin.

The inspired story writer ends this all-encompassing drama with this warning: "If any man shall take away from the words of the book of this prophecy, God shall take away his part out of the book of life, and out of the holy city, and from the things which are written in this book."[9]

This, then, in outline, is the content and meaning of the old Bible of Christian tradition. It is the old Story of Salvation that the Christian church has been telling for more than fifteen hundred years. It has often been called "the greatest story ever told." Men have crossed continents and endured martyrdom to proclaim it to all peoples.

Should this old story be the core of Christian religious education today? Should it be taught as a whole? If not, what should be omitted? How much revision can be made in this "divinely revealed story" of man's destiny and still have the truth in it preserved? What are the values in this old tradition for us today? How much of it can we believe? Does it express our faith? Shall the whole Story of Salvation be told to children in Christian churches and only half of it to Jewish children? At what age is it fitting to tell either the Christian or the Jewish versions of the story?

6

The Bible — Newly Interpreted

> We consider bibles and religions divine — I do not say
> they are not divine;
> I say they have grown out of you, and may grow out of
> you still;
> It is not they who give the life — it is you who give the
> life;
> Leaves are not more shed from the trees, or trees from
> the earth, than they are shed out of you.
>
> — WALT WHITMAN

HOW DOES THE NEW BIBLE, as it is being reinterpreted to our generation by Biblical scholars and students of history, differ from the old Bible of tradition?

As we have shown, the old Bible was so interpreted as to present one unified and consistent story beginning with Genesis and ending with Revelation. Men go to the old Bible to learn about God, his purposes, his commands for man, even to learn God's thoughts and feelings toward man. The old Bible is conceived of as primarily a revelation of divinity. It is "God's Word."

The Bible newly interpreted, as a result of our new knowledge, is shown to be a collection of records of human experiences. It is about people. It tells us what they were like and how they believed about God and their world, and how these beliefs affected their living. In short, whereas the old Bible is thought of as divine, the new Bible is human.

Whereas the old Bible is thought to contain a unified system of religious beliefs, the new Bible of human experience is admittedly a collection of books written by authors who not only lived in different times and places, but whose religious beliefs and ethical standards differed markedly from one another. To study the old Bible means to learn the basic beliefs of the traditional Christian or the Jewish religion. To study the new Bible of human experience means to make a comparative study of a number of different religions. For example, Abraham and Jacob carried images of their family gods with them as they traveled from camp to camp. They also prayed to spirits dwelling in certain trees and springs. Thus while in the traditional Bible story, Abraham leaves his home in the idol-worshiping city of Ur in order to be free to worship the one true God of all the earth, in reality he was himself a polytheist and used idols in his worship.

In the old Bible, God instructs Moses to build an ark in which the tables of the law might be kept, and where God's presence would always abide. The archaeologists, however, have found evidence to indicate that there were probably many such sacred boxes — perhaps one in every Canaanite shrine as well as in every Hebrew shrine. Praying before an ark consisted of asking a question of divinity that might be answered by "yes" or "no."[1] The answer to the prayer was secured by casting lots. Furthermore how different the religion of Job was from that of the authors of the Book of Kings and the Book of Chronicles! How much superstition prevailed even in the society in which Jesus lived: belief in the demonic origins of sickness, belief in the efficacy of animal sacrifices in gaining divine forgiveness!

To study the new Bible one must be prepared to examine different beliefs and practices and codes of ethics. There is no one message of truth pervading the entire collection of writings. Furthermore, the Bible books, for the most part, were written by Hebrews and consequently they are all more or less colored by their nationalistic point of view. The Hebrew people generally regarded themselves as the "Chosen People." God is presented as telling Moses to say to his people: "If ye will obey my voice . . . and keep my covenant, then ye shall be a peculiar treasure unto me above all people."[2] This idea of being especially chosen by divinity to perform a superior role among nations is a concept that has been held by almost every nation in the world at some time during its history. But our ancestors accepted the Hebrews' estimate of themselves as a "Chosen People," unique among the nations; and the whole Story of Salvation was woven around this idea. When the Hebrews rejected Jesus as their Messiah, the Christian church took for itself the title the "Chosen People of God," and thus injected into Christianity, in spite of all its claims to universalism, an exclusiveness and a self-righteousness that have poisoned Western civilization ever since.

Archaeologists, excavating in the Near East and elsewhere, have finally made intellectually untenable the idea that the Hebrews were the first monotheists of history or that they were a peculiarly religious people.

For example, Dr. Breasted in his *Dawn of Conscience* has shown that in Egypt "the Sun of righteousness rose over two thousand years earlier than he did in Palestine." In the ancient Memphis Drama, dating far back in the fourth millennium B.C., there is pictured "one God," the creator of all that is, the original Mind and Heart of the Universe — a belief which seems very similar to the Logos of the Gospel of St. John. Describing these priests of Memphis, Dr. Breasted writes, "They see the world about them functioning intelligibly and therefore conclude that it was brought forth and is now maintained by a great all-pervading intelligence, which, by a touch of pantheism, they believe is still active in every breast and every mouth of all living creatures."[3] Be it remembered that these Egyptian priests lived almost three thousand years before Amos or the Second Isaiah, and more than two thousand years before Moses.

Nor were the Canaanites as inferior religiously to the Israelites as the old Bible presents them. A number of buried cities within Palestine and Syria have recently been unearthed and it was discovered that a great civilization flourished all over that country centuries before Joshua and his tribesmen invaded the land. Even in Abraham's time there were walled cities of no mean proportions, and the art in ancient Canaanite temples is now regarded by some scholars as fully equal, if not superior, to the contemporary art of Egypt. In fact, these despised Canaanites were the Phoenicians, the inventors of the alphabet. When they were robbed of their great kingdom and were squeezed into the small country around Tyre and Sidon, they retained their virility and became the skilled navigators of the Western world.[4]

Not many years ago a number of Canaanite poems were discovered in Ras Shamra in Northern Syria. These are dramatic epic poems and songs used in the Canaanite temples during the period when Abraham and his people were wandering shepherds. Some of the Biblical Psalms resemble these ancient Canaanite psalms so closely that it is probable the Hebrews copied from their neighbors. In these poems one Creator and Ruler of the universe is praised, and other gods are mentioned as intermediaries. According, then, to the light shed by the findings of the archaeologists, the differences between the religion of the Hebrews and that of the Canaanites have been greatly exaggerated. Both worshiped with images, male and female. Both sacrificed animals and slaves and even children on their altars. Only a few great prophets of Israel and a small number of unknown and unusual persons rose above the sexual excesses in their temple rituals, and revolted against the cruelties of war and the injustices of a city civilization.[5]

Nor can the ethics of the Hebrew people be set off as so peculiarly above the standards prevailing in other nations. The Code of Hammurabi and the Negative Confession of the Egyptians both merit favorable comparison with the Ten Commandments, even though they are much more ancient. A still earlier code of the Sumerians, recently come to light, may well add to our appreciation of the high moral character of other ancient peoples as well as of the Hebrews.

Furthermore, the ethical standards presented in the Bible are conflicting. On the one hand, "to do justice and to love mercy and to walk humbly with thy God" is set forth as the whole duty of man: yet on the other hand, slavery, national exclusiveness, race hatred, cruelty, stealing, murder and war are all justified by men presumably speaking for God. No intelligent person can go to the Bible to get one clear answer regarding what is right and what is wrong. The various standards have to be examined, and valued in the light of the larger cultural setting in which they arose. No longer can authority for the teachings of the Bible be derived from the Bible itself. The worth of one ideal above the other depends on the value judgments of the reader who wishes to compare present ideals with those of men of the past and so to gain more insight.

The new Bible, as interpreted by Biblical scholars, is avowedly a combination of myth, legend and historical record, mingled together without discrimination. All the records were made during a period when miracles were commonly believed to occur, and before men had conceived of the scientific concept of a law-abiding universe. Consequently the natural scientists and modern students of history have influenced us in our interpretation of Biblical history. A neo-orthodox theologian may describe Bible history as "salvation-history" and say we do not go to the old Bible for real history; but such a distinction can have no useful meaning for most serious students. The religion of a people and their history are inevitably woven together. To study them separately robs both the history and the religion of their truth. If historical or scientific facts are twisted in order to set forth certain religious ideas, the validity of the religious ideas is shaken.

Because the Bible records were all made before the scientific concept of a law-abiding universe had taken hold of men's

minds, the Biblical narratives abound in miraculous interpretations of events which seem unreal to the modern mind.
It is again and again assumed that God manipulates the
forces of nature much after the manner of a commander-in-
chief of many armies. These natural forces are the tools of
God's personal will. Sometimes they are his weapons of wrath
and sometimes they are the means of his special blessing and
approval. He holds back the waters of the Red Sea or of
the Jordan River in order to help his "Chosen People"; and
he floods the valley of the River Jabbok in order to bog down
the chariot wheels of Sisera's hosts. Even Jesus is represented
as having the miraculous power to still a storm, to walk on
water as if it were solid land, and to bring Lazarus back to
life after his body had lain in a tomb for three days. Not
only is Jesus' own resurrection portrayed, but it is written, in
Matthew 27: 52 and 53, "that many bodies of the saints that
had fallen asleep were raised; and coming out of the tombs
after his resurrection they entered into the holy city and appeared unto many." Such an astounding story could be believed by Christians during the second century after Jesus
lived, but modern man, whose whole thinking about this universe is scientifically conditioned, cannot believe. Even the
elementary school child, who is experimenting with nature's
laws, has to discount such stories.

In the old Bible Jesus, the Jew, is portrayed as a supernatural being, born of the union of God with a virgin, to be
the Savior of the world. His death was divinely permitted, and
his resurrection from the dead was the final proof of his
divinity. Biblical scholars have been struggling for a hundred
years and more to untangle from these ancient accounts the
actual facts regarding the person who once lived and taught
in Galilee. They have suspected the inconsistencies in the
different Gospels as revealing later traditions which modified
the facts to fit contemporary theological beliefs. These men
have been on a patient quest to find "the historical Jesus."

They have been asking: What sort of a person could he have been? What was the burden of his teaching? Why did the Jews and Romans regard him as a dangerous disturber of the peace? Did he think of himself as the Jewish Messiah? Did he foresee the founding of a church in his name? Did he lay stress on what was believed about him?

From these long years of persistent delving into the Gospels and into other contemporary reports, which tell of conditions in the Near East during the period when Jesus lived, scholars are now presenting an impressive picture of a dynamic and creative religious teacher. They are finding a man who not only had an outlook on life and religion markedly different from that of the Pharisaic leaders of his generation, but one who had a point of view that was in profound contrast to the religious assumptions of the churches that now worship him. In the new Bible of human experience there walks a new Jesus — not a divinity desiring worship, but a man who can be understood, honored, and in deep ways followed.

The new Bible, as reinterpreted by Biblical scholars, is considered in its historical context. Its history, its religion, its ethics and its science are seen as old and in certain ways different from ours today. To be sure, some of the old is still true. There are universal feelings and ideas and experiences to be found in these records which appeal to intelligent and good people as being still true to life; but these are the jewels that must be searched for. Until the assumptions representing what is narrow and prejudiced and unscientific are clearly recognized for what they are, and are separated from the wisdom, the use of the old heritage in educating the coming generation cannot but impede our progress.

When the overlay of tradition is removed, however, and the actual human experiences are seen as the thoughts, feelings and deeds of real people, both great and small, the Bible is transformed into a different sort of book from what it was to our grandparents. Instead of being a world drama of salvation planned and carried out by God himself, it becomes the human drama of one people, Israel, containing the recorded memories of their outstanding religious prophets and teachers.

Although these facts regarding the new Bible, as interpreted by Biblical scholars, may be known to the readers of this book, we cannot assume that the rank and file of the citizens of our country or even of the teachers in our Sunday schools and synagogues are aware of the contrasting meanings between the old Bible and the Bible newly interpreted. This ignorance is due to the fact that in most popular religious literature, the distinctions between these two points of view are not clearly drawn. A kind of lip service is paid to the findings of archaeology and Biblical criticism, while the general and important basic ideas in the old Bible are still assumed and taught. The old Story of Salvation is still being told in most of the churches of Christendom. To be sure, some of the portions most difficult to believe are omitted. Many of the miraculous events are glossed over or evaded while at the same time the most important miraculous events are assumed as true, with no effort being made to give sound evidence for them other than the fact that they are part of the Biblical story. The churches and the synagogues seem afraid to set forth the issues clearly.

Dr. Leroy Waterman, when president of the Society of Biblical Literature and Exegesis, in his presidential address chided his colleagues for their ineffectiveness in educating the rank and file of ministers and church members regarding the nature of the new Bible of Biblical scholarship. He dramatically pictured the kind of world we would be living in if the physical scientists had been as ineffectual as the Biblical scholars in popularizing their findings. If the scientific findings of the past one hundred years had been "frowned upon and ignored to the extent suffered by Biblical investigations," he said:

For one thing, officially, we should conceivably still be living on a flat earth, regarded as the center of the universe. Men might, to be sure, have traveled around it and scholars generally would have little doubt about its form, but this would scarcely have gotten into the textbooks and those who openly declared its rotundity would be looked upon as radicals and as somewhat queer — if not dangerous.

The discovery of the power of steam would have been known, but without encouragement or practical support, it would have been very difficult for that knowledge to get beyond the teakettle stage; and with that limitation it is questionable whether the modern development and wide use of steel would have been possible, and consequently we might very well still be in the age of the ox cart and sailing ships.

The transmission of the human voice over a wire by means of electrical impulses would doubtless have been known as an interesting curiosity. But under the repression and public disapproval at every divergence from accepted usage, could the Atlantic telephone ever have come into being?[6]

Some unobtrusive but powerful influence has indeed restrained professors of the Bible, ministers, rabbis and writers of popular Biblical books from speaking out frankly and fully regarding the changes that new scientific knowledge has made in their attitudes and beliefs regarding the Bible. The professors have been absorbed in the details of exegesis, while many editors and writers of children's Bible story books have assumed apparently that accurate scholarship is unimportant when dealing with the Bible and children. The result has been that matters of crucial importance have been left untouched — matters involving the very foundation stones on which the old Story of Salvation rests. Both groups seem to be afraid of becoming involved in the serious process of change in religious thinking and teaching that the emergence of this new Bible has made necessary.

The old Bible seems simpler to relay to children because of its unity and because of its certainty regarding God's ways with man. The new Bible, as interpreted by Biblical scholars, is more difficult. To appreciate it, children must be old enough to have discovered that mankind has had a long history of development, that people of long ago could not think as people do today. There must be enough maturity of mind for the child to be able to visualize certain historical settings out of which the stories came. Young people of today should feel the common human bond between themselves and these people of long ago, yet they must be able to grasp why the religion of former times cannot be ours. Although they will recognize that in all ages and countries, men have felt dependent on invisible powers and have yearned and struggled to gain greater security, justice and peace, yet young people will recognize also that many of the old patterns of belief and life do not belong in the society of today. The responsibility for discernment between conflicting ideas and values is thus laid upon the child.

In the present state of confusion, it is sometimes difficult for amateur students of the Bible, such as librarians, parents, book reviewers and teachers, whose work is primarily with children and youth, to understand just what the issues are, and to make the needed distinctions between the theologically biased Story of Salvation (the old Bible), and the book containing the records of human experience from which to gather the historical facts regarding one nation of the old world (the new Bible, as interpreted by modern scholarship).

In order to be practical at this point, it may be useful to suggest a few test questions which an adult may ask regarding a particular book of Bible stories or set of lesson materials:

Is God represented as speaking and acting as one of the characters? Or are the characters all human beings who wonder about God, or who are puzzled to explain events?

Are myths and legends presented as if they were historical facts? Or are they told as stories people have imagined in order to explain some puzzling or extraordinary event?

Are the stories told to teach children what God is like, what he wants of them and what he forbids? Or are the stories told to let children know what people of long ago were like, how they thought of God, their ideas of right and wrong, and their ways of praying so that children may compare or contrast the old with the new and decide which ways are best?

Is it assumed that the Hebrews of the Old Testament worshiped the "one true God" and that the Gentiles worshiped false gods or idols in contrast to the Hebrews? Or are both Hebrews and Gentiles presented as using images in their worship, and as praying in quite similar ways, each hoping for favor from their gods?

Are the "men of God" in the Bible portrayed as doing miraculous things? Or are miracle stories presented as the interpretations given later of extraordinary but natural events?

Is Jesus pictured as one with supernatural powers, as one chosen by God to perform a particular mission revealed miraculously to him, and as one who knew beforehand that he was to rise from the dead? Or is Jesus presented as a natural person with human limitations, always learning, sometimes uncertain of what he should do, a man of superior character and insight?

How any given book of Bible stories or lesson materials deals with such issues as these will determine whether it represents portions of the old Story of Salvation or whether it represents the Bible reinterpreted by Biblical scholarship. The one book will portray as facts supernatural activities and events, as well as myths and legends; the other book will be a thoroughly human and natural record.

Having, then, these two contrasting possibilities in dealing with our Judeo-Christian Biblical heritage, religious education has a complex and difficult situation to face. Which Bible should the children of our time come to know: the drama of God in history as conceived by the church fathers and based largely upon the general pattern of thought bequeathed to them by the Hebrew prophets? or the dramatic story of the Hebrew people, struggling and suffering and achieving, retold in the light of the fullest modern scholarship available? Or do children need both Bibles? How relevant is either story to the life of children today?

7

The Need for Both Bibles — and More

Limit not thy children to thine own ideas. They are
born in a different time.

— THE TALMUD

HOW SHALL THE BIBLE BE USED in church and synagogue
schools today? If it is studied as a human book, as the source
material available from which to gain a knowledge of the
history of the Hebrew people and their great prophets, shall
it continue to be used as our one major source of knowledge
of man's ancient religious experiences? If the Hebrew people
is no longer correctly regarded as religiously unique above all
other peoples of ancient times, should our children spend
as much time as is customary on the history of this one
people to the exclusion of that of all other peoples? If Jesus
is regarded as a very great religious genius or spiritual leader
or ideal personality, rather than as the "only begotten Son
of God" or as the one divine Savior, are there other great
spiritual leaders of ancient times whose lives and teachings
should also become familiar to our youth? Where should the
emphases be placed? How shall choices be made? These are
questions that need straightforward answers, if we can find
them.

To substitute for knowledge of the past, mere hostility
toward the old is surely not an adequate solution. "To rebel
emotionally against one's past is not to transcend it," writes
Dr. Floyd Ross, "but is to bind oneself to it by inversion.
Rebellion can become an occasion of growth, but it is never

87

growth itself." [1] To try to solve our present problems in the light of recent human experience alone is a shallow solution, and indeed a dangerous one. Today's problems have their yesterdays, and to understand the particular forms these problems take today one needs to know their yesterdays.

We are not, however, merely the "bellhops of history passing the baggage of one generation on to another," writes Dr. Angus MacLean. "Culture makes it possible for human relations to bridge the grave, for individuals who are so short of days to live with a wisdom derived from the dawn of time. Our job is not to worship history and culture like fetishes, but to feed them into our living, creative stream of personal life for spiritual and intellectual reprocessing." [2] No ignorant enthusiasts — neither those who would excite men to return to "the old-time religion," nor those who would repudiate all that goes by the name of religion as if it were outmoded — can help our generation in this time of change.

But how can such breadth of understanding and wisdom be engendered by a study of the Bible — either of the old traditional book or of the book as reinterpreted by students of history? Loyalties and affection for the old treasures hang like a mist before our eyes, and tend to blur our ability to be objective and discriminating; and fear of having what is distinctive in the Christian or the Jewish faith unappreciated or perhaps even destroyed compels most religious teachers to be evasive.

In our own experience, a group of sixth-grade children opened our eyes. We had stood staunchly for postponing all Bible study until children were old enough to be able to enter imaginatively into historical situations different from the present ones in which they had personal experience. Such an attitude we still regard as sound. In our present culture children usually begin some elementary study of history, beyond that of their own immediate environment and country, during the fourth, fifth and sixth years of school. It seemed to us appropriate, therefore, to expect children of nine, ten and eleven to become curious to learn also a little of the history of primitive man's beginnings in religion.

But we recognized that the Bible as a historical record of experiences is a difficult book even for adults to understand. Furthermore, the Bible has the disadvantage of being the historical record of but one people, and we were eager that our children should discover early in their historical studies the universality of our common human urge to understand the meaning of life and to find a way of co-operation with the intangible powers about and within.

So for two years previous to their entrance into the sixth grade we had been leading these children over wide pastures. They tried to find out why and when the most primitive of peoples began to be religious. We imagined stories of the cave people 20,000 years ago: we built our stories on the conclusions drawn from cave paintings and other artifacts of early man, found in France and Spain. The class studied also two groups of primitive folk now living, the Bushmen of Africa and the Aborigines of Australia. We had gathered from other lands stories of how people had prayed for rain, and why they had felt that certain springs and rivers were sacred. Some of the class had found legends from the Northwest Indians. They discovered how these Red Men had reverenced animals and learned how they interpreted the meaning of dreams. The children were told several stories of creation, not merely the two found in Genesis, but stories told by such differing peoples as the Chinese, the Greeks and the African Pygmies. In fact, these children had traveled in imagination to all the world's continents, going from the present back into the ancient past. We wanted them to realize how naturally religious beliefs had developed, to know that all human beings have the same deep yearnings and face the same major problems in achieving our desires. We had hoped to instill respect for primitive peoples who, in spite of their ignorance, had so courageously led the way in experimenting with the invisible and unknown elements in existence. We wanted the children to feel that it was just as adventurous and exciting for men to learn to make prayers as to learn to make arrows and boats. Our ambitions were far greater than the results, but a beginning had been made.

Finally, when entering the sixth grade, the children said, "We've been studying about other people's religion. Now we want to know our own. We want the Bible." So we took the children at their word. The class began studying the Bible, beginning with Genesis. Naturally the teachers dealt with the experiences of these Biblical folk in the same manner in which they had dealt with the experiences of these other peoples the children had previously studied. They gathered what concrete data they could from the ancient Bible records and combined these with the added information available in books written by Biblical scholars and archaeologists. The children questioned the supernatural interpretations and the theology that was assumed in the Biblical narratives, and they tried to figure out what could really have happened, and how these beliefs had come to be. Although our efforts were awkward and our imaginations were often stilted, yet the people of the Bible began to grow real and understandable to the children, and they could identify their feelings with those of long ago.

But this kind of a Bible was not what these children had expected to study. They soon sensed the fact that once more they were studying how primitive peoples of long ago had thought and felt and done, whereas the children had asked to study "our religion." As the weeks passed we found their interest lagging. They were disappointed, and so were we.

"You asked for the Bible," we said, "and now that you have an opportunity to study it you are not interested. What's the matter?"

"We thought we were going to find out about our own religion," they said, "but instead we are just studying about the religion of these ancient Hebrews!"

How right they were! And how inadequate our own thinking had been! The children had been told (by others than ourselves) that the Bible was "The Book" about the Christian religion; that in it they would learn the truth about God; but they had found it was about ancient beliefs which somehow were not very different from the beliefs of the primitive people they had already studied. So we stopped then and there and tried to explain to the children the reason for their disappointment. We contrasted the Bible as it had long been understood — the Bible containing the one great story of God's plan of salvation for mankind — with the Bible as it is now understood by those who have studied it in a scientific spirit. In order to help clarify this contrast, we spent one full hour on the old Bible story, presenting it in much the same way as it is given in Chapter 5 of this book. This rendering, however, proved to be too condensed for children of eleven to grasp fully; yet even the little we did seemed somehow to clear the air of some of the confusion and bafflement that the children had experienced.

The following year, when a similar situation arose in another class, we tried again. This time, instead of spending one Sunday, we took at least six Sundays in telling the children this old Story of Salvation. Since the lengthened story gave opportunity for vivid details, the whole drama became more interesting. The children felt the suspense and the tragedy, the terror as well as the strength, the cruelty as well as the majesty in it. After each section was read the children would talk it over. They were led to feel free to say whatever they thought and to ask any question they wished to ask.

As the drama progressed the children recognized stories from the Bible which they had already heard, but had never before seen as parts of one great drama of mankind's destiny.

They recognized phrases occurring in Negro spirituals which they had sung without understanding, and they discovered the meaning of certain billboard signs such as "Jesus saves."

The children gathered up some of the large ideas in the whole story which seemed to be still true, and set over against these ideas other thoughts in the story which seemed to be false. Some of the children wished the whole story could be true. Others were afraid it might be true; and still others were sure that a great deal in it could not be true. To think about these things demanded vigorous mental activity and straightforward emotional expression.

One class made a long mural depicting the Seven Great Ages of Time. Another made a stained glass window and painted seven scenes on it. Two other classes danced the rhythm of this drama of human destiny, in contrast to the rhythm of the story of evolution.

All the while as the children worked over the story in their imaginations, they kept wondering and questioning. In every instance someone from outside was asked to meet with the class, the minister or some other person whom the children thought could help them clarify their thinking. The following questions are samples of the queries the children raised.

"Did Moses really have a staff which he could tap things with and make things happen, like the water coming from the rock?"

"That lady couldn't really have turned into salt. I think that perhaps Lot's wife might have fallen into a salt pit, and that was how the story got started."

"If we don't believe that a person could turn around and become a pillar of salt, how can we believe in the evolution story that says that animals turned out something else?"

"If men did do these things, how did they get the power?"

"How much of the story of Salvation is really true and how much is fake?"

"How can you tell what is true and what isn't true?"

"Can God do anything he wants to?"

"Was Jesus really the Son of God? If God did not have a wife, how could he have a son?"

"God isn't a person. He's a spirit. How can he have a big family and how can he grow?"

"Did Jesus really live? How do people know?"

"Do you really believe that Jesus healed the sick? How can you prove it? I know the Bible says so but you can't say that everything the Bible says is true."

"Do you really believe that he came back to life after he was buried?"

"What's Jesus' resurrection got to do with us, anyway?"

"How do you know that Jesus turned those little fishes into enough to feed all those people? It's just a fairy tale."

"God always seems to be angry in this Story of Salvation."

"It seems that God is always picking out certain people to be his favorites."

"If nobody can see God, when he came down to earth what did he look like?"

"How do we know that there will be an end to the world like that?"

"Why don't the Jews believe in Jesus?"

"Was Jesus afraid to die?"

"Did God know who was going to turn away from Jesus in the end?"

"Why do we have people go to other parts of the world to tell this story?"

"Who made God? How did he begin?"

"If there was always a base — how did it start?"

Thus, although we began with the old religion of our ancestors, we always ended with some of the most profound questions regarding "our own religion."

When the Story of Salvation was completed in one of the

classes, a boy reported his feelings at the home dinner table. "Mother," he said, "we finished the Story of Salvation today. You know, I'm so glad we had those other stories first — you know, those creation stories from Japan and China and Africa, and from the American Indians, and the scientists' story of evolution — because if I had heard this Story of Salvation first I would not have known *how to think about it.*"

Thus the boy sensed the reasonableness of the educational process through which he had been privileged to go. One condition for religious freedom is exposure to more than one way of thinking and believing. The ability to grant such freedom requires in the educator a respect for children's ability to think and a trust in the power of truth.

As a result of these experiences, we came to the conclusion that sometime during the progress of their religious education, children in our Western culture need to be vividly exposed both to the old Story of Salvation and to some portions of the Bible as reinterpreted by modern scholarship. Without knowing the Story of Salvation in its old and unexpurgated form, no one can fully appreciate the power and persistence of certain basic assumptions that permeate our Western ways of living and feeling. No one can be free from the mistaken and divisive concepts that have been collected in the debris of our social history for two thousand years unless he realizes how old these ideas and feelings are and from what sources they have come. Moreover, if one is unaware of the kinds of treasures that may be mingled with the gathered dust of the ages he may, in his ignorant digging, destroy much that is of high worth.

This ancient Story of Salvation still lives in our literature and art, our music and our rituals. There never would have been a Christmas or an Easter had it not been for this great story. Ideas from it appear again and again in the hymns and Christmas carols children sing. What do these words mean to them: "Born a king on Bethlehem's plain"; "The little Lord Jesus"; "Cast out our sin and enter in"; "Born the king of angels"; "Come, thou Almighty King"; "Father, all glorious, o'er all victorious"; "In the cross of Christ I glory"?

That the children in most church schools ask so few questions about the meanings in such songs as these suggests an unpromising dullness of interest. If we had kept their minds more wide-awake, they would have openly expressed their restiveness; they would have wanted their confusions cleared away. They might not have slipped out of our churches. A frank and full rendering of this old Story of the Bible in its original dramatic form serves to give young people an orientation into the culture in which they live. Such a study, of course, should be combined with an open and fearless discussion of the ideas that permeate the story. These should be compared and contrasted with present-day philosophical and scientific thought.

There *is* a greatness in the old Story of Salvation. Our ancestors had their spirits lifted by it. As John Burroughs said, it healed their wounds; it developed character; it tempered the steel of their natures. "It was an heroic creed." Merely to cast it all aside as totally incredible is foolishness. There must be some worth in it, else it could not have inspired so many millions. Not a few of the details, presented as facts, are clearly false. It is the great "truths," as the neo-orthodox say, which are contained in the narrative that it is important to discern; but it is equally important to discern those assumptions that falsify life. The whole structure of the plan of salvation was worked out during a time when kings ruled and subjects obeyed, when it was believed that wrongdoing must be avenged by punishments and goodness especially rewarded. Our generation is breathing a new intellectual and emotional atmosphere. New philosophies are being expressed in modern poetry and drama, in the modern novel and modern art. We see emerging a new cosmology, new attitudes toward right and wrong, and a new vision of a world-wide, democratic community.

To suggest changing such a long-lasting and, in its time, such a valuable religious system of thought as is contained in the old Story of Salvation is an extremely difficult task and also a dangerous one. One finds many evidences that a struggle is going on. It is a cautious movement. There is fear lest, in improving the structure, the foundations may be blasted. Emotional tensions run high.

These are not problems merely for theologians. They would be of great concern to all sorts of people if they were made aware of the issues that are being raised. Everyone, in a measure, must be a theologian. Whatever may be the outcome of the religious turmoil in which we are living, it is of great importance that all who teach should be aware that our religious culture is changing. Our children have to face this general fact.

They need a security also that can give them the courage to help in making changes in spite of the persistent and powerful resistance to change that characterizes religious organizations. Since it is so important that religious educators should see clearly what the issues are and the reasons why changes are being called for, we shall devote the next three chapters to a detailed examination of the contrasting conceptions in the old and the new cosmologies, the old and the new moralities and the old and new dreams of humanity's future.

Teaching "the Bible" to children, then, can no longer be looked upon as a simple task, that of spreading intelligence regarding a series of more or less interesting Bible stories. Nor can the present generation of youth be content merely to know the old Story of Salvation, and the meaning of its emotional and intellectual penetration into the life of the Western world. They will need also the corrective that can come only through some understanding of the true history of the Hebrew people in contrast to the theologically biased conception of God in history as portrayed in the old Story of Salvation. They will desire also to know the historical Jesus, what he really did and taught, in contrast to the picture of the supernatural Christ of miracle and omnipotence. In how much detail and how completely this generation of youth will care to go in knowing this Biblical history is a matter that can be learned only in co-operation with young people themselves. We can be quite confident that some portions, at least, will make a strong appeal.

Naturally when the uniqueness of the Bible has been removed and it becomes an ancient historical source from which to glean an understanding of the experiences of one national group, children will ask: Why then should we not learn of other peoples also? Were the Hebrews the only religious people of ancient times? Why should we not learn of other great religious teachers as well as Moses and Jesus? Thus the door is wide open, leading into a study of the universal experiences of mankind in building religious faith and practice. This means that this generation of youth will be asking for more than both Bibles — the old Bible and the reinterpreted Bible. They will become curious about the world's other Bibles as well. As humanity seeks one common human brotherhood, embracing all religious cultures, and differing religious beliefs are exchanged freely and sympathetically, we may discover the great ways in which we are all alike, and thus we may see our differences in their true perspective.

Indeed, the pursuit of this natural and reasonable approach to religious guidance has led the author to the conviction that the universal note should be heard even at the very beginning of a child's education, and it needs continuing emphasis during the pre-adolescent years, as well as during all of life.

Most teachers of religion would persuade children very early in life to become little Christians, or Jews, or Buddhists, or Mohammedans. Later during adolescence, perhaps, they would permit young people to study other religions. But first of all, they would have the children well grounded in their own religious heritage. We have been experimenting in another way. We believe that children need first to have religious feelings of their own; that they need to be themselves religious before they can be good Christians or good Jews or the followers of any specific faith. Children should *feel* the Mystery of life, before being told how it has been explained. Children should *feel* the wonder, before being given the words to say it by. Children should *feel* a trust, before being told that there is a God on whom they can depend. We believe in taking the young child's own questions, at their true and deep worth. Who am I? What is everything about? We would recognize children's questions as their real childhood prayers — put into the language they know how to speak.

And as children are led in imagination into the past, we would help them to see that all over the world, in many times and places, people have been saying the same kinds of prayers. They have been trying to understand the world in which they have lived. They have recognized that there is more to the world and to life than the eyes can see. Even the Pygmies of Africa and the Aborigines of Australia sensed "the intangible at the base of finite existence," and they worked out their own experiments in order that they might feel united with the sources of spiritual energy.

Some teachers have feared that children, when beginning to study man's history, will be confused if introduced to a variety of religious beliefs, especially primitive ones. We have found through our experience, however, that the variety in itself stirs children to deeper appreciations and feelings, and that the experiences of primitive peoples have a directness and closeness to nature that children can understand. When exposed to different ways, children are obliged to dig beneath the verbal forms and rituals to find the common feelings with which they can sympathize. When children are given only one belief as taught by one person of authority, or when they are taught one way to pray, it is easy for them to equate the forms with the reality. They are prone to assume that the Mystery has been explained and no further exploration is needed.

As never before in history, the world needs those who can feel spiritually related to all kinds of people. Knowledge of our religious heritage is indeed important, but that heritage comes down to us from all quarters of the earth. No one can prophesy from which ancestral line some fresh insight may come.

A class of ten-year-olds had been reading and discussing a number of myths of creation told in a score or more of national groups and primitive societies. They had also studied the modern scientist's story of evolution.

One day Richard complained: "Why do we study about all these people? We ought to be learning about God. We almost never say anything about Jesus. I don't see why we come to Sunday school."

In response Allen defended what the class had been doing: "It's this way," he explained. "Here in this Sunday school we go the long way around. We find out about all these different ways people have thought, and then after a while we will come back to our way in this country. This seems slow, but I like it better than the other way because I want something to put Jesus on top of."

Although some of us would not be so sure as Allen was that Jesus would have to be on top, yet we can surely sense the soundness of his reasoning. If Christians really hope that Jesus will come out on top, comparisons must, at least, be permitted. As was illustrated in Chapter 2, such teaching by simple affirmation and authority tends to develop authoritarian children, with hostile prejudices against those of a different point of view.

The religions of the world are all changing. Whatever our

inherited faith, we all have the same fundamental problem to struggle with, to change and to re-create our inherited religions in harmony with our changing concepts and attitudes toward our universal home and our destinies within it. We need to clear away our confusions and our narrow prejudices, and to join hands in the greatest and most difficult quest man has ever begun. A new religious era is emerging from the womb of yesterday, and our youth should be intelligently prepared to help in its birth.

8

Old and New Cosmologies

I say the whole earth and all the stars in the sky are for
 religion's sake.
I say no man has ever yet been half devout enough,
None has ever yet adored or worshipped half enough,
None has begun to think how divine he himself is, and
 how certain the future is.
I say that the real and permanent grandeur of these States
 must be their religion,
Otherwise there is no real and permanent grandeur;
Nor character nor life worthy the name without religion,
Nor land nor man or woman without religion.
 — WALT WHITMAN

EMBEDDED IN THE STRUCTURE of the old Bible is an ancient
cosmology or philosophy of the universe. This cosmology is
not presented abstractly in broad generalizations, such as are
found in the catechisms taught to young people of former
generations, but it is hidden in the simple guise of the dramatic
Story of Salvation where even a child may discover it.

What then is this old cosmology? How does it differ from
our modern cosmology? And how important are these differences to a modern child's religion? At least six of the
characteristics of the old cosmology bear directly upon our
answers to these questions and deserve our serious consideration.

The picture of the earth and sky as presented in the old
Story of Salvation is recognized by all Biblical scholars as
primitive. To the writers of the first two chapters of Genesis
the earth was comparatively small and flat with the dome of

101

the sky revolving around it. Fastened to this moving dome were the sun, moon and stars, and above the dome was a sea of waters, which were released from time to time upon the earth by means of windows in the dome which could be opened and closed.

Above these waters was heaven, the abiding place of the Creator and Ruler of the earth; and with him dwelt a company of holy angels who served as his messengers to man. Beneath the flat earth was Sheol, the dwelling place of the Prince of Darkness and his associated demons. All events both on the earth and in the sky were controlled from outside and above the cosmos by this Creator who could look down through the sky's transparency and see all that happened and who occasionally would come down to the earth himself to accomplish his purposes.

It is important to remind ourselves of this cosmology since in its main features it continued to be satisfactory to most of the Western world until the sixteenth and seventeenth centuries when it was challenged by Copernicus, Kepler, Galileo, and other great forerunners of the scientific revolution. Today, however, such a simple conception of the cosmos is an impossible one for even an elementary school child.

The lure of scientific achievement is strong in our times. Thousands of children are being taken to our great planetariums where the solar system is demonstrated for them, and they are led to wonder if human beings live on Mars. Furthermore, the sun is shown as but the nearest of all the stars. Then as the child begins to look for himself, perhaps through a junior-sized telescope, at the star-dotted sky or at the moons of Jupiter, he asks more questions. His imagination is stretched toward vaster and vaster realms. He will learn later what our great telescopes are revealing about the nature of the Milky Way, our own galaxy, with perhaps one hundred billion suns in its whirling disk, many of which probably are centers of other solar systems.[1] Sooner or later the child educated in our culture is bound to hear of the great 200-inch telescope on Mt. Palomar. He will find out how astronomers estimate from the evidence of actual telescopic photographs that unnumbered other galaxies are scattered over the vast spaces beyond our own, reaching at least a billion light years farther into the depths of space.[2] Unimaginable figures for any mentality!

How can a child learning of such immensities help but speak disparagingly of a belief in angels who can fly back and forth with messages from God who lives in a realm beyond and outside all this unspeakably vast cosmos? Traveling at the speed of light, it would take an angel more than 100,000 years to fly across even the diameter of the Milky Way — to say nothing of the vaster regions through the other galaxies beyond.[3]

When we turn from a consideration of the heavenly bodies to examine the old and new conceptions of life upon the earth, there is an equally dramatic contrast. In the Genesis stories, not only is the earth the center of the universe, but man is the center of all creation. All forms of animal and vegetable life were created for man's special benefit and were intended to be under his control.

We cannot but smile at the conception that on a certain day or in one ancient period long ago, God created all the species of living creatures that now inhabit the earth, together with all forms of vegetable life, both those that now flourish and those that are now extinct. In the Biblical story, further- more, we are told that samples of all these living species were not too many to be gathered into a single ship that sailed the waves of a world-wide flood. In view of the more than one million already known and catalogued species of animals now living on the earth,[4] it is no wonder that Noah's ark has become a Walt Disney comic and a child's toy.

Today such naive and simple understandings have been replaced by a general acceptance of the theory of the evolution of life from non-living matter. There may be a legislature here and there or an ecclesiastic organization that still denies to children a clear understanding of the implications of this theory. It is difficult, however, for most children to escape these assumptions of astronomy, biology and zoology which permeate our society and not to recognize that they contradict the old cosmology of Genesis.

Why, then, does it continue to seem important that these ancient accounts of Genesis, in which this primitive cosmology is found, should be told to young children among their first Bible stories — even before they hear what the scientists have learned about the beginnings of earth and sky and of life itself? There seem to be at least three reasons. First of all, many children at an early age ask questions about first things and who made them. Even though many scientists assert that it is futile to try to find out a First Cause, the child often asks for one, and religiously minded parents are eager to give the best answer possible. The Bible says: "In the beginning God created the heaven and the earth"; and the stories of Genesis naturally follow.

To those who regard the old Story of Salvation in the main as true, these stories are of strategic significance. Man's creation in the perfect image of God and then man's fall from grace and his defilement through the sin of disobedience are the very cornerstones of the entire plan of salvation. When the "truth" of these stories was first challenged by Copernicus and Galileo and later by Darwin, it was inevitable that violent protests from religiously minded people of the Western world should have followed.

There are Christian and Jewish leaders today, however, who now regard this conflict between science and religion as resolved. They point out that the science in the Bible must be distinguished from the "spiritual truths" it reveals. These "spiritual truths," they say, children should early come to know. The simplicity of the cosmology, it is believed, makes it possible for children of five and six to grasp the stories and accept the lessons in them. The fact that young children are so easily impressed adds further assurance to the Bible story-tellers.

Other leaders, who have rejected the cosmology in these Bible stories, and even perhaps some of the basic "spiritual truths" in them as well, have still another purpose in telling these stories to young children. Their reason is that it is important that children should be introduced early to the Bible as "great literature." It is said that children should know these stories for the same reason they should know other classical stories within their grasp.

This was the point of view in one church where these stories were regularly told to six-year-olds. The teachers were instructed to answer frankly any questions the children might ask, but the teachers were not to raise questions themselves. For one child, at least, the experience was unfortunate. Although in the classroom she had listened without comment, she showed her irritation on reaching home. "I don't want to go to Sunday school ever again!" she complained. "Why, what happened?" asked the mother. After the child had explained what she had learned from the story of Adam and Eve, the mother said, "Don't be so worried, Mary. I don't think your teacher believes that story is true either. She would call it a myth."

"Then why did she tell it to us?" asked Mary. With the clear insight and the realism of a child nourished in freedom, this young girl put her finger on the basic question: Why then tell these stories to such young children?

In contrast to these ways of transmitting ancient Biblical beliefs to children, it would seem much more reasonable first to expose them little by little to the nature of the universe in which they live as this is conceived by intelligent people in their own generation, and later to let them know how people long ago used to think. A scientifically accurate picture, although but vaguely drawn, is better than one made incorrectly concrete or one framed with primitive ideas which the child necessarily must destroy to make room for the expansion of his understanding. To build the beginnings of faith in God on a conception of the universe that our generation no longer regards as true is to prepare the way for a loss of respect for the Bible; and what is worse, to court a cynical atheism when the child is old enough to learn for himself.

The modern child, long before adolescence, is called upon to develop a maturity of courage that many of us who are grown have not yet achieved. Children in our grade schools are really living with "nature's immensities." They need a philosophy of life that will enable them to "stand cool and composed before a million universes."

Having noted the contrast in the general pictures of the cosmos and of life as presented on the one hand by the Bible story and on the other hand by modern astronomy and zoology, let us turn to some of the more serious questions. Let the story of Adam and Eve be accepted as myth; and the six days of creation treated as symbolic of the five hundred million years it is supposed to have taken, according to the theory of evolution, for the present number of living species to have come into being.[5] Yet, it is said there are certain great "truths" to be found in these prescientific stories. Let us then look at these "truths" and ask: Does modern thought challenge these "truths" at any vital point? If so, has it anything better to offer?

I

First of all, we note that one of these general ideas or "truths" in the old Story of Salvation is that the Golden Age was in the beginning. God pronounced everything he created as "good." Even the first man and woman were pure and without sin. From this initial stage of perfection and happiness, mankind and all nature with him have desperately fallen.

The general trend of the Story of Salvation is downward until the coming of the Savior from heaven. Evil, pain, labor and death were required to discipline man and bring him back to his original goodness, but all these proved inadequate to man's desperate need. According to the Story of Salvation, God alone can change the downward trend. This idea that man is so weakened by his sinful nature as to be left incapable of learning to live a good life is the very foundation on which the need of a supernatural intervention rests.

In contrast to this look to the past for the ideal and to this despair of man's native abilities, the story of evolution leads us to look toward the future with hope. Instead of pessimism, it awakens a respect for the potentials not only in man but also in all forms of life. No scientist today doubts the truth of the fossil records in the rocks of the earth. Although the trend as set forth in the story of evolution is not one of continuous or inclusive or inevitable progress "onward and upward forever"; nevertheless, as thus far enacted in history, it is a record of astounding progress for certain branches of living creatures, and it is a promise of further possible progress still to come.

II

Closely linked with this idea in the old Story of Salvation that the Golden Age was in the beginning is a second so-called "truth": that God's creation was completed during the initial period.

In contrast to this conception of a completed creation is the modern idea of a cosmos that is continually re-creating itself. Some years ago there were scientists who predicted that the universe was running down. They pictured a doomsday when everything now in existence would be dead. Today, although it is still recognized that portions of the universe are apparently running down, it has been discovered that an opposite process is also going on. Dr. Fred Hoyle of Great

Britain has recently brought forth evidence, apparently convincing to many other scientists as well as to himself, that the universe is continually growing. It is not merely expanding like a balloon, but it is actually adding to its own substance. By proposing a mathematical theorem and then making tests to see if it worked, Dr. Hoyle believes he has discovered the actual rate at which new matter is being created — so many atoms of hydrogen to so much space.

When asked: "Where does the created material come from?" his answer is: "It does not come from anywhere. Material simply appears — it is created. At one time the various atoms composing the material do not exist, and at a later time they do." A very strange idea, he admits, "but in science it does not matter how strange an idea may seem so long as it works." Apparently, then, creation of the material cosmos was not completed "in the beginning" but is continuous.[6]

In the realm of living things, also, as we know them on the earth, new forms are being continually created. Instead of the idea that all species of animals and plants were once and for all determined in the first period of creation, there is rich evidence to show that new species are continually coming into existence. So-called higher forms of life are still emerging from lower forms. Modern man does not have to go back to the beginning to find a Creator, because he finds evidences of the work of a Creator or of a multitude of creators in the here and now.

Research workers have been studying the conditions that promote the creation of new species. Scientists have been experimenting to find ways by which they can control the direction of evolution. Their first experiments have naturally been with very simple and fast-reproducing living things. As a result of many long and painstaking experiments, it has been found that the trend of evolution can be directed by changing the environments in which the genes of the male and the female unite. Man can influence the survival of certain mutations and can speed their growth. He can provide opportunities and stimuli for new creations. But the actual ability to create new forms is lodged within the very seeds of life, the sperms and the ova and even more minutely in the genes and chromosomes that the seeds contain.

At this point modern science has recently been revising the popular interpretation of the Darwinian theory of evolution which held that new mutations are produced by a process of mere chance, a shuffling of the cards marked "genes." Opinion now seems to be moving toward a recognition that there is within the living organism itself a dynamic which can best be described by using such words as "a faculty of invention"[7] or "a creative response."[8]

"The joy of living, the desire to live, the will-to-live — these are what breathe in everything living, from the lowest cells to the highest organisms, and account for their behavior."[9] So writes Dr. Charles Mayer, a French scientist. Dr. Theodosius Dobzhansky of Columbia University writes that "evolution is a creative response of living matter to the challenges of the environment. The role of the environment is to provide opportunities for biological inventions. Evolution is due neither to 'chance' nor 'design'; it is due to a natural creative process."[10]

How this entire creative response began in the first place, if there ever was a first time, is a continuing cause for yearning wonder. The mind of man seems never willing wholly to abandon its effort to reach out in imagination toward Infinity. Nor would it seem wise to discourage children from these wonderings. Each one must needs try to plumb this mystery for himself. Instead of reducing children's appreciation of this Creation, we would rather increase a child's reverent eagerness by encouraging his direct awareness of the evidences of creation in the here and now.

The ability of children to grasp something of the significance of these immediate findings is shown in the following conversation between brother, sister and mother.

Nine-year-old John and five-year-old Jill were reaching out in their childlike way toward this basic mystery within the universe. It was spring. For some time gardens and babies had been their chief topics of conversation. Finally one day, as the two were sitting in the living room alone while their mother was in the kitchen with the door open between, Jill said to her brother:

"When you plant a bean it just grows and grows into a bean plant and it has little beans and roots and everything. John, how does it know *how* to grow into a plant?"

"You plant it and the sun shines on it and the rain waters it. That's how it grows," said John, the young scientist.

"But," said Jill, "the sun doesn't know it's supposed to be beans. The seed is under the ground. If we planted a bean and it grew carrots we'd be surprised. Somebody must know how it is supposed to be. I guess it must be the bean that knows."

"Well, I don't think the bean *knows* anything," said the young scientist with assurance.

"Then Daddy and Mother must know," said Jill puzzled. "I guess that's how it is."

"Daddy and Mother couldn't possibly know anything so wonderful as how to make a bean plant grow from a seed," said the mother peering through the doorway. "We only know how to plant the seed. We only know that if we plant a bean and the sun shines and the rain falls, then it will grow into a bean plant. That's all anybody knows."

Jill persisted. "Babies would be harder to make than beans. You and Daddy know how to make babies grow."

"Oh no!" said the mother. "We only know what to do so that the baby can start to grow. It is like planting the seed. We didn't know anything about you at all until *after* you were born. We didn't even know whether you were a girl or a boy!"

"But you knew I was *me!* Didn't you?"

"No. We're just getting acquainted with you as you grow. We will never know *all* about you."

Jill was baffled. "Then how did I get to be *me?*" she asked.

"The same way a seed gets to be a plant, I guess," said the mother. "It is wonderful, isn't it?"

"It must be God that knows how," said John rejoining the discussion. "That's what God is! *God is what knows how to grow.*"

In this short final sentence, John summed up the new and significant insight that replaces the old idea of creation by God's fiat of a completed and perfect world once and for all in the beginning. Jill sensed that the mystery of the boundless creativity permeating the universe is to be found in even the seed of the bean. After all, the bean seed in some way really does *"know"* how to become a bean plant, and in this creative growing life John recognized God as "what knows how to grow."[11]

The great philosopher, Dr. Alfred Whitehead, expressed in mature language what these two children discovered for themselves. "God is the intangible fact at the base of finite existence."[12]

III

A third belief expressed in the old Story of Salvation needs basic revision in the light of modern thought. This is the belief in a clear-cut distinction between the natural and the spiritual worlds, between mind and matter, an idea which has resulted in a lack of respect for the material world.

According to the old Biblical cosmology, man's habitation is in two distinct places and is of two different kinds. The material is temporal, a place of pilgrimage; the spiritual is eternal, co-existent with God. One is natural, the other supernatural. Many theologians even today consider the testimony of the natural world regarding the nature of God as unimportant and, some would say, misleading. For centuries, many Christian people have equated nature worship with heathenism.

Linked with this traditional point of view is another significant belief, namely, that the natural and the spiritual are enemies. "The world, the flesh, and the devil" have long been the demonic trinity. It was said that man must escape his material bondage. The worst that many theologians even yet can say about our modern culture is to call it materialistic. The Christian world has long looked down upon the material as partaking of the sinful nature of fallen man. This idea stemmed from the story of Adam's fall, for God is said to have cursed the ground (in the Latin Vulgate the word used was "terra," meaning the whole earth) as a punishment for this first disobedience, and made it bring forth thistles and weeds, thus requiring man to gain his living by hard labor and by the sweat of his brow. In short, man would have to struggle against the natural world and conquer it.

This curse upon nature led to many anxious discussions among the church fathers. It was indeed a frightening conception and so influenced Western thought that English poets were not able to write of the sublimity of mountains until the eighteenth century. Mountains were long thought of as "warts" and "wrinkles" on the surface of the earth, signs that it was "growing old like a garment," in accordance with God's curse. Luther was terrified of mountains, not enthralled by their grandeur.

To our modern thought, this disparagement of the material world and of material things seems in a sense immoral. Dr. Oliver Reiser of the University of Pittsburgh writes: "Philosophy no longer requires the dualism of 'matter' and 'spirit.' Body and mind are two poles of one organism; matter and spirit the two poles of one universe."[13] If we respect one, we must respect the other also.

Doctors of medicine and psychology have had to accept the unity of the person in body and mind. It is probably no more exact to speak of the mind or spirit as living in a body than it is to speak of a body as living in a mind or spirit, for both mind and body seem to be essential parts of one life.

Physicists and biochemists also have been obliged to recognize that the boundaries between their respective fields of study are slowly disappearing. The dividing line between the living and non-living can no longer be drawn clearly. On the basis of experimental observations, the biologists are inferring that bacteria have feelings.[14] If so, do viruses also have feelings? At what stage do feelings begin?

The time was when scientists thought that the basic building blocks of the universe were particles that could be seen and measured if only strong enough microscopes could be invented. But the more they see, the more the mysteries seem to increase. Matter that once was thought to be something tangible, that could be touched and seen, is now believed to be energy at comparative rest; and energy is found to be matter in excessive motion. Matter and energy are one and the same. What then is matter? And what is energy? Furthermore, this energy-matter everywhere is apparently electrical in character. It is also known that "electricity is produced wherever there are living cells."[15] Wherever there is life there is electricity. Can it be that wherever there is electricity there is life? It is becoming increasingly difficult to answer. The mystery in an atom of matter parallels the mystery in a seed.

It seems that no matter into what phases of the material world research leads, the seeker sooner or later meets the invisible, the intangible — some would say the living and the "spiritual." These intangible phenomena, however, are part and parcel of the material world — both animate and inanimate. It no longer seems unreasonable, therefore, to suggest that the universe as a whole as well as in its minutest particles may be alive. This is a very old conception both among Eastern and Western philosophers. Many great thinkers have characterized this universal and all-pervading vitality as God. Today advancing research seems to be leading us back to an appreciation of this ancient thought.

Modern man, whatever his interpretation of modern scientific thought, can no longer set himself off from nature, for man is part of the natural world, and the material of the earth and stars is in him. To deny the worth of the physical world is to deny our own worth. Our material and spiritual destinies are inextricably mingled. Nor can modern man think of God as commanding him to subdue the earth and to "have dominion over the fish of the sea and over the birds of the heavens and over every living thing that moveth upon the earth."[16] Scientists are developing a growing respect for all living things, and have discovered that *co-operation with nature* rather than *ruling over* it leads to humanity's larger good.

We live in "one world" where not only are all men "brothers," but the total cosmos is one interdependent unit in which all the smaller units from man to animal, from vegetable to mineral, and on down to the tiniest particles of electrons and protons, mesons and photons in the cosmic rays, are of one kind. Altogether we are a unified cosmos.

> Nothing in this world is single;
> All things by a law divine
> In each other's being mingle.[17]

This Life that permeates all our existence some think may well be called God. In this Life we live and move and have our being.

IV

A fourth so-called "truth" in the old Story of Salvation is the answer given to the question: "How is the cosmos controlled?"

In the old Story of Salvation the forces of nature are controlled by an Almighty Personal Being who uses these forces of nature as a means of moral discipline. God sends storms, floods, earthquakes, pestilences, famines, in order to punish evil-doers. He also grants special blessings, such as rain on needed occasions and increased fertility to flocks, and general prosperity to those who obey his commands and worship him alone. God takes sides by special intervention in battles between nations, helping some by drying up rivers or by making the sun stand still; while others he destroys in his righteous anger by torrents of rain and by death-bringing plagues. The entire order of the universe, according to the old cosmology, is dependent upon the will of an Almighty Guardian of morality who uses his power to deter mankind from evil by rewarding obedience with special favors, or by punishing wickedness with trouble and destruction.

The scientific conception of the universe as acting with regularity, according to certain enduring laws, is clearly contradictory to the conception of any arbitrary suspension of these laws for the purposes of moral discipline. All forms of miraculous intervention by a divinity from outside the natural order to change the working of the very laws attributed to his divine planning are becoming more and more unthinkable to more and more people. Modern man finds in the very working of these natural laws a wisdom so profound that it appears to him irreverent to believe the Creator would change them arbitrarily. Dr. Lawrence Frank writes: "All our historical conceptions, of nature and of social life, were built upon this same pattern of power, force, cause, authority which controlled and directed whatever happened, told man what he could and could not do, speaking as deity, king, emperor or as boss. . . . Today we have a new conception of the universe as self-governed, and self-regulating, interrelated and interacting to the farthest reach of space-time."[18]

Such a statement does not imply a denial of a Creator. Nor does it mean that this cosmos is a chaos without control, meaning or purpose. It does, however, mean to those who are now attempting to absorb this new conception of the universe that unbelievably great powers of control are within the very nature of existence. They are lodged in the ability of the cosmos, taken as a whole or taken in its minutest units, to be active, to create the new, to grow and to evolve. How these amazing powers of creativity came to be there in the first place, none can know; that they are there, all can observe.

If then we try to think of these powers of creativity, collectively and inclusively, as unified, and we call this Creativity and Self-renewing Power by the time-honored and noble name of *God,* such a God is immanent and natural, rather than transcendental and supernatural. Modern man has discovered such majesty and glory and power within this cosmos that he is inclined to agree with Dr. John Macmurray's comment that "What our childishness thinks of as another world, a supernatural world, is merely the reality of this world which is hidden from us by the imperfection of our own sensitiveness."[19]

Such a conception of the universe and of God is so different from the traditional Western thought of God as "entirely other" and as belonging in a supernatural world, that many moderns have felt obliged to discard entirely the use of the word *God.* This seems unfortunate. So great a thought and so deep an emotional response to the cosmos as a unity needs some kind of symbolic expression. If we can continue to use the word *God* for this new belief it keeps unbroken the bond that unites us with the long line of deeply spiritual leaders and saints of the ages. For we too are still searching as they also searched, and we too continue to feel the ineffable Mystery which they felt.

What is needed is not a new word, but new thinking and new feelings, shared without evasion. We need to revise the definition of God given in standard dictionaries, and we need to accustom ourselves to living with new thoughts and feelings in relation to God.

All this is extremely significant for those who are teaching the young. It means that children must be given their own firsthand opportunities to read the Book of Nature, using both the spirit and the techniques of science, so that their ideas and their feelings may expand and deepen.

V

Another important conception that is gaining weight among scientists is that the universal natural order resembles a democracy more than an autocracy or kingdom. The old Story of Salvation emphasizes conquest and dominion while biologists and other scientists are finding a balanced interdependence between all things which can better be described by the word co-operation.

During the past few decades, the theory of evolution as propounded by Darwin has been somewhat revised. Instead of the commonly accepted conception that evolution is promoted primarily through an individualistic struggle for existence, with the conflict resulting in the survival only of the fittest, it is being shown that paralleling this universal urge to struggle to preserve individual existence is an equally strong urge to co-operate. In spite of all that has been said about nature "fierce in tooth and claw," there seems to be manifest, even in the first evolutionary steps, a fruitful balance between a readiness to co-operate and a desire to preserve the individual life. It was, after all, unicellular living creatures that first tried co-operation. The existence of higher animal forms are living proofs of a persistent urge to co-operate and a readiness to experiment. It would seem that we have good reasons for being proud of our animal ancestry, perhaps more than we have for being ashamed of it.

Five hundred million years ago one-celled animals and plants were alone on the earth. They were bumping and pushing individualists, each seeking literally its own place in the sun. In some way, shall we say "by choice," a different possibility was found. Some "chose" to join together. This momentous step led to many more possibilities. Larger and larger groupings were made. The cells organized, divided up their functions, became specialists. Other living units "chose" to remain separate, or to limit their unions to small aggregates and simple organizations. As a result of these millions of years of such ongoing new creations and experiments in co-operation, life today is multitudinous and varied, the simplest earliest viruses surviving alongside the highest animals.

During these ages some forms of co-operation became static and the process of evolution was thwarted. This occurred when too much was surrendered by the individual cells; for example, when the reproductive powers were relegated to a very few members of the species, as with bees and ants. Other forms of organization proved to be dynamic, and from these forms man slowly evolved. Human beings in their turn have exhibited the desire for larger and more complex socialization, while at the same time they have tried to protect their separateness.

When the struggle for individual existence is seen alongside the parallel tendency toward co-operation, it takes on a fresh meaning. "No reasoning is necessary for a bacterium or a plant to know that it is a good thing to live," writes Dr. Mayer.[20] "All things live by the faith that the struggle is worth it; they have done so from the beginnings of protoplasm," says Donald Culross Peattie, the naturalist.[21] What fascinating ideas on which to meditate! Every tiniest bit of living thing feels it is good to live. Can it be that even in the lowest living forms there are the beginnings of a feeling of worth, a principle which among human beings represents something that is basic to democracy?

Instead, then, of an evolution which is primarily a process of competition and warfare between differing forms of life, with the strongest surviving in the struggle, the process becomes one of balancing the two basic and valuable urges within all living things — the urge to preserve the individual life, and the urge to be joined with other life forms. Evolution would have been impossible without this balance between freedom and socialization. It is because such large numbers of living things once found greater enjoyment in uniting their forces than in remaining separate that the evolution of more complex and more capable creatures was possible.

"Through many laboratory experiments and observations in the field," says Dr. Ashley Montagu, "we are being shown that we have been close to 100 percent wrong in thinking of animal life as a dog-eat-dog existence." [22]

VI

Finally, we come to the last and perhaps the most significant and revolutionary of all the differences between the old and the new cosmologies. It will require the questioning of an idea which for many Christian people is the very foundation stone on which their religion rests. This is the traditional belief about death and immortality.

According to the old Story of Salvation death came into the world as a punishment for man's sins. It has, therefore, been something to be afraid of, an event that has evoked a feeling of guilt. Often people experiencing the coming of death into the inner circles of their affection cry out in their anguish, "What wrong have we done, O God, to deserve this punishment!"

Such a concept of death as the greatest of God's punishments upon man is distasteful to those who have accepted death as a natural companion of life. It is in marked contrast to the attitude of Jesus toward death, which he saw not as something to be escaped, but as the very condition of life. When his disciples were bemoaning the prospect of their Master's death, he said these unforgettable words: "Except a grain of wheat fall into the ground and die, it abideth alone; but if it die it bringeth forth much fruit." [23]

Furthermore, since in the old Story of Salvation death is pictured as a punishment hanging like a shadow over the consciousness of every human being, it becomes the great motive in the drama of human life to escape this condemnation.

And how may death be escaped? It cannot be escaped in this existence. Bodily death continues to be the common lot of all. It is, then, a spiritual resurrection in a spiritual eternity that is the goal. And this is made possible for those who accept the promise implicit in the resurrection of Jesus Christ, described by Paul as "the first fruits of them that sleep." To make this point doubly sure, St. Paul wrote to the Christians in Corinth: "If Christ hath not been raised, your faith is vain."[24]

The old belief in death as a punishment is in marked contrast to the thought that death is a natural consequence of life. Without the death of individuals, evolution would have been impossible, and the monotonous existence of changeless forms of life would be the dull alternative. When one is able to accept a long-time view such as this, death can be regarded as a blessing rather than a curse.

Emerging in our culture is an awareness of everlasting life of another kind than the one described in Revelation. It awaits everyone here in this universe. Hard as it is to imagine, nevertheless it seems to be true, that what we have been and done will make a difference, even though a very small difference, in all that will come hereafter. Such a thought is in line with the belief in the unity of all existence. If this interplay of forces, this inevitable giving and receiving, goes on between each individual and the totality in so commonplace an activity as breathing in and out, what shall we say of other more intangible activities through which we are continually receiving and giving away? Is there an end to this interchange?

What is an individual apart from these relationships? We give the seeds of life, and new personalities are born from them, while we experience what is called death. The new generation grows to manhood and womanhood. They surrender the seeds of their life, and still another generation is born. Thus life goes on and on. Forms change, but Life breathing through all the forms survives. Life has already risen from the dead for every one of us a million times and more!

And whose life is this? It is yours as well as mine. It is mine as well as yours. There are no favorites in the everlasting life. As individuals with faces and names and characters we disappear; yet there may be that which never disappears. One wonders. Is there ever an end to the years of our lives here in this universe?

Other equally yearning questions may be asked. Was there a beginning to us? Can we name dates when we began? Because we have personally forgotten what happened before we were born, does this mean we began only with our memories? What are the instincts that condition us if not forgotten habit patterns, established through millenniums of practice by living people whose life is within us? Who can count the millions of mothers and fathers who have given us the life we call ours?

We cannot escape the thought that all the yesterdays of time are somehow living in today. And today will somehow live in all the tomorrows of time to come. Time is already eternity. We need not move to another world to find eternal life.

Such thoughts may seem strange to those for whom they are new, and they may be to some forbidding. A revamping of the traditional Christian philosophy seems to be called for. Even to examine these emerging beliefs in our culture means that we must ask new questions. Not what belief about death and immortality does the church teach, and what belief will give the most comfort and inspiration, but rather what belief seems to be true to our deepest experiences and our richest understanding of life.

The old and the new cosmologies differ indeed in significant and vital ways. Our expanding knowledge of the universe, our convictions regarding the reality of evolution, our reaching out toward a belief that Life in some mysterious way permeates this universe, that the creation of the new and the better is a possible reality, that all is unified, that the spiritual and the material are but differing forms of one basic reality, that our animal heritage has in it greatness we had not surmised, and finally our discovery of new meanings for death and immortality — all these require a courageous analysis of the old Story of Salvation.

Surely certain of the old treasures deserve preservation. Some very great ideas and qualities of thought in the old Story of Salvation still remain unchallenged. Although the characteristics ascribed to God in the old and new cosmologies differ, yet the basic belief in some unifying power on which all Life is dependent still remains on which to build anew. There remains also the dramatic picture of the long and arduous struggle to achieve the richer values for life. The sweep of the old Story dramatizes the need in every generation for mature and noble leaders who can lead and inspire groups less mature than they. The perspective of the Story of Salvation is that of eternity. Our present generation needs the ennobling of the long-time view.

Most people have not given these matters serious meditation. Many have gone no further than to disavow the old tradition. They have been left wistful, feeling unsupported by religion, and yearning for a security that cannot be shaken. It is time to become more articulate with our thinking, to lift the curtains of reserve, and to remove the fear of plain speech lest we be cast out by our churches, or be rejected by our friends or lose our means of livelihood. The call is for a fundamental remaking of our major cultural pattern.

For adults, if considered apart from the younger generation, this basic revolution in our faith and cosmology may be postponed as not too important. It would cause more emotional disturbance and practical sacrifice than the majority can endure. But for the young, who have not yet been emotionally bound by the old traditions, it is of untold importance that they should be given the opportunity to grow up as integrated and whole persons with their religion and their science harmonized. Without this harmonizing, they will be crippled with a kind of religious infantile paralysis, with one leg dwarfed while the other grows to adult stature. With such uneven development, they will not be able to walk with firmness and poise the highroads of the new age.

9

Old and New Moralities

Whom shall I fight and who shall be my enemy;
Where he is I and I am he? . . .

   Let me have done with that old God outside
Who watched with preference and answered prayer,
The godhead that replied
Now here, now there,
Where heavy cannon were
Or coins of gold!
Let me receive communion with all men,
Acknowledging our one and only soul!
   For not till then
Can God be God till we ourselves are whole.
     — WITTER BYNNER

BEFORE THE AGE of psychoanalysis and psychotherapy, the *physical* scientists were the ones who shook the foundations of Western religion. First the astronomers enlarged our cosmos to overwhelming proportions so that no intelligent person can now be dogmatic regarding a cosmic God. Then the biologists changed man's meager conception of time with the hypothesis of evolution and thereby destroyed the foundation stone on which the simple Christian drama of creation and salvation was built — namely, the truth in the Biblical story of creation. Then came the biochemists and physicists who delved with amazing results into the microscopic world of the molecule, the atom, the neutron, the meson, down, down toward smaller and smaller units of reality. They have shocked us with their vision of power in the unimaginably small. They have found the intangible in matter itself, an imponderable that holds our worlds together or can burst them

124

apart. Again and again we have been required to readjust our thinking and our feelings toward the cosmos. As a generation we are swept along by a swiftly moving current of momentous discoveries, yet we still struggle to hold to some kind of religious faith or philosophy of values.

But great and difficult as are these adjustments, demanded of us by the scientists of the physical universe, even more searching and difficult changes may be called for by the findings of the psychological scientists or the psychotherapists. These scientists have at last entered the realm to which liberal leaders of religious education once retreated — the realm of moral and social living. And they are exploring the emotional or inner life of the spirit, the area that the great mystics have thought of as peculiarly religious and beyond the range of scientific search. Although this new science of the emotional life is in its beginnings and although there is considerable disagreement among the various schools of psychoanalysis, yet there is already appearing enough agreement and conviction among them to challenge both traditional and liberal religious education. An operation even at the very heart of our liberal faith is being asked for. Let us then go back once more to the old Story of Salvation and look particularly at its assumptions regarding "good" and "evil," and how the "evil" can be changed into the "good."

Throughout the old Biblical drama, the contrast between "good" and "evil" is sharp and clear. It embraces all time and space and reaches beyond to include even divinity and eternity. God himself is the symbol of perfect goodness and the Devil is the symbol of utter evil. When Adam and Eve yielded to the temptation of Satan, the conflict between good and evil began, and the first strategic victory was won by evil. During the First Great Age of Time the war between good and evil became so severe that it ended with God's destruction of mankind in a world flood and his beginning again with Noah and his family, the only "righteous" group. Again evil became so powerful that God separated from the nations one "Chosen People" to bless and help: but again and again this "Chosen and Separated People" sinned and were finally scattered in exile. At last came the divine Savior — the Son of God himself — and by accepting his goodness as a substitute before God for man's badness, a remnant was to be saved.

Usually when this story is retold today, the great emphasis is put on the boundless love of God in granting salvation, rather than on his disapproval and punishment of all unrepenting sinners. As a result of this emphasis on divine love, another significant theme running through the whole story is blurred. This theme expresses the very meaning of man's existence, namely, that life on earth is an unending conflict between two forces, one symbolized by God, and the other symbolized by the Devil. The outcome of the conflict is assured, but there will be no surcease in the war until Time has passed away.

This then is the ever-recurring motif in this tragic symphony of life. God is ever trying — over and over again — to help mankind to defeat evil. Yet evil continues to defeat good. The one great issue for every human being is to decide between these two powers. On which side will he take his stand — with God or with the Devil?

Religious liberals have rejected this traditional Story of Salvation at its most vital theological core — the supernatural nature of the world Savior. For decades the Unitarians have been emphasizing "salvation by character" rather than by supernatural intervention. This was a significant and courageous step made necessary, we think, by advances in scientific method and knowledge. But having made this radical revision of the old Story, liberals have too commonly thought they had done all that was needed. Without realizing it, however, many have not yet rejected an equally important implication in that ancient interpretation of history — that man's life on earth is an unending battle between good and evil. We are often quite unconscious of how deeply this idea permeates our thinking, and how powerfully it affects our emotional relationships with one another and within ourselves.

This conception creates in many of us a kind of compulsive feeling that we must fight *for* people and causes that are good and we must also fight *against* all that is wrong. Like the prophets of old, we must condemn wrongdoing and we must punish the wrongdoer. He must be crushed or be made helpless or cast out of our society. It is this basic concept and attitude toward good and evil that the psychotherapists say has been shown to be untrue to the real nature of man. It is a point of view that holds us back from making the progress we all theoretically long to make toward a united and more harmonious world.

Let us consider another implication in that old Story of Salvation. How long does this division between the good and the bad last? The answer is "forever." And how does the warfare end? The answer is "By the unconditional surrender of the wicked." They are crushed under the heel of the Messiah; they are punished by a fire that never destroys; they are cast forth, even out of the sight of God. The Christian tradition gives no hope of a united humanity even in eternity. We should never forget our indebtedness to the Universalists for their rejection of this everlasting moral dualism.

Furthermore, the conflict as set forth in this Biblical story is not merely between good people and bad people or between God and the Devil. There is war continually even in the inner life of every person. We are told that we have inherited two natures: one divine, the other demonic, and these natures within us are in continual conflict. The good self we call conscience; its desires and its judgments are the voice of God within. The other self, our evil nature, also speaks to us, but we should obey only the good voice. We should cast out all evil thoughts. We should push them away where we can forget them. This philosophy of dualism does not merely divide mankind into two warring groups. It divides our very selfhood into two opposing natures. And it divides our deity also. Instead of there being one God for all life and all humanity, there comes to be one god of the good and another god of the bad.

To convince ourselves of the extent to which we are still influenced by this warring concept of life, we need but to examine our hymnology and our prayers. "We must fight the good fight." "We are soldiers of the cross." "The Son of God goes forth to war, a kingly crown to gain. His blood-red banner streams afar. Who follows in his train?" "Who is on the Lord's side?" "Christ is our captain in the well-fought fight." How frequently in our conversations and in our public addresses relating to modern social and political problems we use the simile of war. "We must fight for this reform." "We must fight against this other party or group." We must even "fight for peace"!

Such an attitude makes it inevitable that we divide the people of the world into two camps — the good and the bad, our friends and our enemies. Whenever such categorical divisions are made, we begin to see our side in an idealistic light and the other side in the most despicable darkness. Clear distinctions are necessary when the spirit of fighting prevails. Wherever a state of war exists, mutual respect vanishes. Rule by authority returns, and with it comes its twin offspring, reward and punishment, praise and condemnation.

The whole ethical atmosphere of this old Biblical drama is out of harmony with the assumptions on which modern psychiatry does its work. In order that we may realize the deep significance of the changed attitudes represented in child guidance clinics today, let us consider a concrete situation.

Miss Andrews had given her class a period of free activity. Tina had chosen to make a picture.

Miss Andrews stood above Tina watching the swift unhesitant crayon strokes. In nine-year-old sureness Tina had made a nine-year-old come to life on paper, with great round blobby tears streaming from her eyes to the floor. In one hand the picture-child held what was unmistakably a fashionable woman's hat, feathers and all; in the other hand, what was equally unmistakable, a knife. Only, peculiarly, the knife had been plunged into the brim of the hat, tearing a gash neatly across.

Miss Andrews shuddered.

Tina looked up, shifted from one foot to the other, giggled nervously. Half apologetically and half in explanation she muttered, "You see, the girl took her mother's best hat and cut it up with a knife," and then more defiantly, "And she took her jewelry too and threw it in the ocean. . . ."

"Only I don't see the jewelry," said Miss Andrews, for the moment off guard. Quickly, however, she caught herself. After all she was a teacher and responsible for the morals of the young. "Tina," she was gently reproachful, "that's not a nice picture. Don't you think you'd better put it in the wastepaper basket and start all over?" And with kindly encouragement, "I know you can do much nicer things."

Into the wastebasket went Tina's picture and with it her attempt to share what was wrong inside her heart. This was Monday and last Saturday her mother had walked out on her father, taking Tina along. Saturday and Sunday nights she had cried herself to sleep. She didn't understand the whole business. All she knew was that she wasn't going to be with her beloved daddy any more and that there was a hard ache inside her and a feeling of bitter blame against her mother who, she felt vaguely, had made the whole thing happen.

Obediently now she drew another picture — a house with smoke coming out of the chimney in the age-old accepted curlicue pattern and a road leading up to the house in conventional coming-to-a-point perspective. Then the recess bell rang.

On her slow walk across the playground, Tina chewed her handkerchief and twisted it into a hard damp coil. George Washington Carver Thompson walked beside her, his dark face wonderingly intent on the lengthening twist of wet cloth.

And then all at once for no immediate reason, Tina turned on him and cried, "You go away, George Washington, 'cause I don't want any dirty nigger following me around."[1]

At first thought, Tina seems perhaps to be a very unusual child. But is she? Let us remember that in the United States during 1949 there was one divorce for every four marriages. How much tension, or conflict, or subdued despair have these divorces brought to children! But even in the so-called "better" homes that have avoided the divorce courts, how many children have deep reasons for resentment — for hatred of a brother or sister who has seemed to be preferred by one or other parent, for feelings of hurt because of an unfair appraisal of their worth, for rebellion against too rigid controls, for fear of erratic authority! There is probably not one among us, if he would be truly honest with his own past, who has not at some time or other during childhood felt some degree of hate or resentment or sadistic desire to destroy or hurt someone in his family circle. Far more often than we realize, children must come to school with tense feelings and heavy burdens on their hearts. At some time or other all children are somewhat like Tina.

Nor was Miss Andrews so unenlightened as a teacher. The very fact that she had a period when a child could paint a picture of her own honest feelings shows that Miss Andrews belonged among progressive educators. In how many of our church schools do we provide periods for free expression of feelings through crayons or paints? We have been taught that other things are more important — such as gaining knowledge about the people of Bible times, about Jesus, about the church, learning to take part in services of worship, singing hymns and saying prayers. In the short one-hour church school, it is said, we dare not waste our precious time in such play. Children can play at home. Yes, Miss Andrews was to a degree an unusual teacher. She had begun to use so-called modern methods, but she had not yet thoroughly assimilated the philosophy that underlies these methods. Therefore in an unexpected crisis, she reverted to her accustomed attitudes.

Let us examine the episode with more care. Just what was it that Miss Andrews did? How was Tina affected?

First of all, we note that Miss Andrews was shocked. She discovered that Tina was not the "good child" she wanted her to be. Miss Andrews felt that to hate one's mother was wrong. It was contrary to all the ideals she was trying to instill. So she said, "That's not a nice picture," and in saying this she condemned not only the picture but Tina because of her anger. Tina had sensed this disapproval even before the teacher had spoken. Tina felt ashamed. She felt she really had been a "bad girl." But she didn't talk back to her teacher; she obediently threw the picture in the wastebasket, hoping it might all be forgotten when she painted another picture that would be "nice."

But when she started all over to do what her teacher thought was better, Tina realized that she could no longer be honest with her feelings. The real Tina — her original, spontaneous self — had to be covered up by a traditional painting of an empty house.

Probably Miss Andrews was pleased. Here was a good child after all — not really stubborn. Very obedient! And what fine self-control she had shown. She could put on a pleasant face in spite of her anger. Perhaps the class had been talking about self-control. Possibly they had read a story that taught just this, that if you give your naughty feelings no exercise, they will gradually die. Tina then had really learned the lesson. Perhaps Miss Andrews was pleased with Tina's second painting and praised it for its bright colors and its neat design.

But what had happened to Tina's anger at her mother? Had her bitterness really gone? When the child got away from the teacher where again she felt free, her real feelings again came tumbling out. But this time, she did not know what she was doing; and she discharged her resentment at a Negro boy who had probably never done an unkindness to her. But nobody told Tina that this treatment of George Washington Carver Thompson was "bad." Too many other children talked that way to Negroes for anyone to notice her meanness except the boy himself who in his turn was building up his own inner store of resentment that would some day explode on someone else. And all this was done, with the best of intentions, in the belief that Tina was learning to be a self-controlled and loving child!

Let us now try to imagine what a psychotherapist faced with this same child Tina might have done. Suppose she had painted such a picture for him. What would he have said?

First of all, the psychotherapist would not have been shocked. It is not that he would have been indifferent to the destructive possibilities in Tina's anger. But he would not have been shocked to find that she showed it, for he would have sensed immediately that there had been some serious deprivation in Tina's home life, and that her anger was a natural reaction. Tina was trying to protect something that to her was precious.

Of course, the psychotherapist could not have said, "That's not a nice picture," for he would have known that the most destructive thing he could do would be to make Tina ashamed of showing her anger. Instead he would try by one means or another to relieve the child of any fear that he would reprove her, and he would encourage her to reveal her feelings even more fully. Spontaneous emotional expression is the doorway through which a child comes out to tell you about himself. To ask him to close that door means that you are ready to surrender your chance to help him. "There can be no therapy with a child who cannot or will not experience real feeling."[2]

The therapist could not help but respect such a painting. To him it would be an expression of real value, regardless of its colors, or neatness or design. The child had honestly and wholeheartedly expressed her feelings. Without this quality of honesty, no painting has worth.

The therapist might not have interpreted the picture to Tina. He might merely have reflected back to the child her own expressions of feeling, repeating her words after her. "Yes, she took her mother's best hat and cut it with a knife." "She was angry at her mother." "Her mother was mean to her." Probably before long Tina might have said, "That girl is me!" But whether she said this outright or not she would know the therapist understood and accepted her, and she would be encouraged to paint more pictures. He would look to see what each painting said; and all of them would probably be kept in a safe place, where Tina and the therapist could find them so that she might talk them over any time she felt like it.

The painting experience, however, would not be merely an opportunity for Tina to reveal her feelings — a chance for free expression. That step was needed. But the full value of the entire episode would be found in the growing experiences to which this freedom led. Was Tina able to continue to live honestly with her emotions without being ashamed of them? With someone to stand by her who kept on respecting her no matter how she acted, did her own self-respect grow? Could she feel happy and loved? Did her hostilities eventually fade away? Could she take some first steps in friendliness?

Children, especially those who for some reason feel unjustly thwarted in accomplishing their deepest desires, are not helped by adults who act as judges of their conduct or as instructors in moral principles of behavior. More than all else they need friendly and understanding persons who will provide them a chance for interesting activities, who can show them respect and empathy no matter how "good" or how "bad" their behavior may be. Children can more easily be spontaneous in the expression of their feelings when they find adults who can share life with them on their own terms — play their games, work with them in paint and clay. Nothing is so important as to keep the doors open to the child's inner life so that the really vexing problems can be expressed emotionally and examined without fear of shame.

Twelve-year-old Julius and his younger sister, Jean, were talking together. For some weeks Julius had been going to a therapist. Jean was naturally curious and asked him one day what he did when he went to the doctor's office. Then Julius told how he and the doctor played marbles together.

In her amazement, Jean exclaimed: "You mean to say you waste your hour with the doctor playing marbles?"

With dignity but also with a bit of scorn, Julius replied: "We don't waste our time, silly. Why, Dr. K. and I talk about such deep questions, you couldn't understand what it was about even if I tried to tell you."

Returning once more to the therapist dealing with Tina, we can be assured that he would not be content to deal with Tina alone. He would realize that Tina was carrying more than her share of the burden of the conflict between the parents. If possible, he would get in touch with them and help them to see what was happening to Tina. He would, therefore, try to show them that they both came with Tina to school each morning, in her memories and her emotions. And through consultation with the psychologist, the parents might learn how to lighten Tina's burden; and, even though they might still accept their divorce as necessary, they might learn how to give Tina enough of her deepest heart's desire for love, to relieve her of her bitterness.

By this time it is quite evident, even from this one example, that the therapist's ways with children are markedly different from the common ways prevailing in our homes, schools and churches. Are these merely differing techniques, or is there a basic difference in the philosophies motivating the different methods? There is, we think, a fundamental cleavage in the beliefs regarding the very meaning of life. Until we see clearly the nature of these differing philosophies and how they have come about, we shall not understand why church groups have been slower than almost any other group in our society to accept the findings of psychotherapy.

What then is there in the emotional conditioning from our religious culture that is so contrary to what the therapists have learned through their clinical work? A brief summary, even though inadequate, may highlight a few of the most significant points.

1. The psychological scientist conceives of living, spiritually, emotionally and ethically, as an evolutionary process, rather than as a continuing battle between good and evil, controlled by God and Satan. Living is growing, learning, experimenting and discovering. How to become a real person of integrity, usefulness, tenderness and breadth of sympathy is not primarily a matter of obedience to principles or to thou shalt's and thou shalt not's, nor even a matter of knowing the right and being willing to do it. It is not a way of life presented by an authority outside ourselves; it is rather a way of life that develops through a growing understanding of our own basic needs and deepest yearnings, and the needs and yearnings of others.

2. To the therapists, the choices that living calls for are not choices between two set categories of conduct — the "good" and the "bad." Indeed, most psychiatrists shun using the words "moral" or "morality" because these terms suggest these rigid stereotypes. For them the word "moral" implies a belief either in a God who commands, rewards and punishes, or in some other fixed authority. To them living is an art much more complex than such a pattern of two simple choices implies. Good and bad have become somewhat relative terms. The practical situations we face always involve mixtures of good and evil, so the very terms are misleading. Good when? Good for whom? How much of good? How much not good? Life for each one of us has a quality of originality and richness that can no longer be imagined merely in two clear choices.

3. To the psychotherapist, emotional spontaneity and emotional honesty and forthrightness are the most valuable qualities of all to keep alive in a growing person. The child who cannot be helped by another person is the child with whom

no genuine emotional contact can be made. The child who has been shamed so often that he is afraid to expose his emotions, who has learned to cover up his feelings in silence, or who must present a polite front to retain the respect and love of his superiors, is the child who is traveling the road to a neurosis. This must have been in Dr. Brock Chisholm's mind when he wrote: "The training of children is making a thousand neurotics for every one that the psychiatrists can hope to help with psychotherapy."[3]

It is because the therapist believes so strongly in this need to preserve emotional honesty that he never condemns an emotion. He will never say, "You should not let yourself be angry" or "You ought not to feel afraid," for he has learned by much experimentation that emotions cannot be turned on and off at will. We cannot love by command. Nor can we stop hating because it is un-Christian to hate. Our emotions are too close to the very heart of our being to be controlled from the outside. A condemned emotion can be repressed, outward expression of it can be withheld because of fear or shame or the desire to please, but the power of the emotion is not discharged until the person himself discovers new feelings.

4. Even when dealing with conduct, rather than with emotions, the therapist would reduce the "must not's" to the lowest possible minimum consistent with the child's own safety, the worth of property and the well-being of others. In using what is now called permissive play therapy, the limits to the child's freedom are purposely few. While he is angry he needs a way to express his feelings that will not bring serious consequences. For example, he may break a doll but not a window. He may hammer a board, but not another child's head. The therapist would not limit freedom arbitrarily for the child simply for the sake of discipline, but according to the needs of the group of which the child is a part, and the purposes for which the group came together.

5. Nor does the therapist often condemn conduct in order to control it. Instead he tries to learn the reason back of the conduct, the child's motive or the experiences which have made the conduct compulsive or typical for the child. He asks himself, What is the child after? What is he craving? Why does he feel hostile? Why is he stealing? Why does he need to hoard his toys and refuse to share? Why is he isolating himself from the rest? Why does he hit? Why won't he talk? Or why is he always so well behaved? So polite? So generous?

A nursery school director had in her group a three-year-old who was in the habit of hitting and pushing and snatching. Knowing the reason for this behavior, the teacher instead of condemning him, purposely made more opportunities to show the boy in some special way, by a little hug or some extra attention, that she loved him. In another case, a parent was concerned over the selfish behavior of her son in kindergarten. The teacher told her not to worry but to be glad, because James for the first time in his life was not afraid to stand up for his own rights.

These teachers had the therapeutic view. They saw the outward conduct in relation to the fundamental yearnings and needs of the child — the search for affection, the need for a sense of personal worth, the learning to achieve specific skills, and the need for adequate and effective techniques for dealing with life's problems.

6. The therapist recognizes that we all have conflicts within ourselves. Our desires frequently conflict and we must choose between them. There is the basic desire for love and dependency, and at the same time there is an equally basic desire to be an independent person, valuable in one's own right, capable of doing something worthy of recognition. But the therapist does not regard either of these desires as "bad." Indeed they are both of the utmost value in personality development. The problem is not one of fighting either desire. The problem is to work out the appropriate balance between

the two desires, and for no two individuals does the place of balance seem to be at exactly the same point. The therapist has learned through experience that he can trust human nature whenever he can get at the real person.

Conduct that may result when one of the child's secret and basic longings is left unsatisfied, the therapist does not think of as "bad," even though it may be antisocial, irritating and even destructive. He believes the child is not naturally selfish, that his instincts are not by nature evil. The child is not simply trying to get what he wants when he wants it because of pure cussedness; he does not therefore need to be disciplined in order to learn that he cannot always have his own way. The therapist realizes that what the child really wants is something of worth. The child will grow in reasonableness as his fear of being rejected or his deep sense of guilt is dispelled.

7. Since the therapist conceives of learning how to live as an evolutionary process, he respects immaturity in ethics as well as in arithmetic. He knows that a young child's apparent selfishness may be due merely to his lack of social experience. Perhaps the child is having his first contacts with other children of his own age. He simply has not learned the useful techniques of social give and take. He is like a person learning to toss and catch a ball. The teacher does not rebuke such a child for his awkwardness. Nor does she hold up before him a high ideal beyond his reach. Instead she lets him try to learn by experimenting. She may give him suggestions now and then, but she does not expect perfection.

To a therapist a child's learning how to be friendly with others is largely a process of learning the effective ways of interchange under encouraging conditions. What may seem "naughty" to some adults is often merely a mistaken or immature way of gaining something that the child has an inherent right to enjoy. If the child uses techniques that are irritating to the others, such as pushing and hitting, the psychologically trained teacher is likely to suggest some other possible way by which he may gain his real desires. But she will avoid, if possible, direct condemnation of the mistake. When a child is old enough to look at bigger needs than his own, the teacher will try to enlarge his imagination, help him to become conscious of other people's feelings and so enable him to identify himself with them. But she will seldom give him a rule to obey, or a general principle to follow, such as that of always being kind or gentle or good.

These then are some basic ways in which the therapist's attitudes differ from those of the usual religious moralist. Lest some think that changes merely in method are all that are called for, we must examine again the traditional Christian or Jewish philosophy of the meaning of human life.

In the old story of the Bible, the normal person is pictured as one who is divided within himself, who has two natures, the divine and the demonic, which are continually at war with each other. To most therapists today, such a divided personality is neurotic. The whole purpose of therapy is to help a person to become whole, to look at his whole self, and to act with his whole self. Under such treatment a person becomes more and more deeply aware of all parts of himself — that which is conscious and that which has become unconscious, that which he admires and that which he has condemned and tried to repress. The divided person is a weakened person, half a person. The fuller the awareness of the whole of oneself, the greater the power to direct one's life intelligently and usefully.

The therapist believes that there is never such viciousness in any person that it must be crushed, demolished or conquered. Rather what has been thought of as "bad" may be merely an infantile or ineffective way of dealing with life's problems. Unless an adult understands the worth of what the child has been striving for, the child's very finest desires may wither away. The hostile thought or deed, instead of being something to be shamed out of sight because it is of the Devil, is brought into consciousness for the child to understand and to redirect. What once resulted in antagonism may now bring forth love. The therapist searches for the roots that are still buried in the murk and darkness. He would save all in order that the whole may be transformed. A boy once said, "The universe has no wastebasket. Nothing can ever be destroyed. It can only be changed into something else." So it is with the personality. Nothing can be destroyed. It can only be transformed into something else. Even the murk is needed to feed the reviving life.

The therapist's attitude toward wrongdoing and toward persons who commit wrongdoing is not that of one who fights them and means to conquer. It is that of a friend, a doctor who wishes to help the patient to heal himself. A therapist has an attitude of objectivity, combined with a warmth of empathy. He seeks to understand and to help his patient to understand. His patients need healing rather than the sentence of a judge. In this the therapists resemble Jesus, who thought of himself not as destroying life but as fulfilling it, and who thought so-called "bad" people were primarily sick in spirit rather than mere offenders against the law.[4]

If religious leaders and therapists met each other more often with mutual respect, perhaps we might learn together. In a united search we might find a unitary and rich meaning for all life within the cosmos, as well as a unitary picture of the single person. A dualistic deity — each part ruling but one half of life — no longer fits the great and expanded oneness to which in modern times we begin to feel we belong. We want a whole self, in a world that is undivided and in a cosmos that is unitary. This means enlarging our imaginative picture of the Everlasting Arms in whose embrace all may feel secure and live in wholeness.

10

An Old and a New World Brotherhood

> We believe in a fellowship that shall unite man, not in
> bonds of Confucian, or Mohammedan, or Christian love,
> but in the holier bonds of human love, going down, be-
> neath all that separates and estranges, to the principles of
> freedom and understanding; below religions to religion;
> . . . a union, not of religious systems, but of free souls,
> united to build up, on the basis of truth, justice, and love,
> the divine Commonwealth of Man.
> — ALFRED MARTIN

THE GOAL ONE SEEKS is like a distant light indicating not only
the direction in which to advance, but also the road. In the
old Story of Salvation is found an awe-inspiring conception
of human destiny, including the place of each individual
human being within it. This vision of the final consummation
of human history is contained in two scenes, the first taking
place on earth, the second, in the supernatural regions above
and below the earth. First, God's Kingdom of righteousness
and peace is to be established in our present world. From the
City of Jerusalem God's representative is to rule the whole
earth for a period of one thousand years. Then the Old
Jerusalem is to be supplanted by a New and Heavenly Jerusalem. All those whose names are written in the "Book of
Life" are to be admitted into this Kingdom of glory and
happiness. But the unrighteous or those who have not been
"washed in the blood of the Lamb" will be cast out into the
Kingdom of Satan where everlasting woe and suffering await
them.

For many centuries this picture of human fate has both

141

frightened and inspired millions of men and women. Evangelists still describe these scenes of ultimate judgment in order to stir men to repentance.

What does such a belief signify? Is it in accord with modern man's enlightened feelings for human values? Have we a more adequate dream of human destiny? In order to answer these questions let us look more carefully at the nature of this Kingdom of God. Let us note its assumptions and its values, and compare them with what our modern generation is beginning dimly to see in its dreams. What are the salient characteristics of the Kingdom of God in the old Story of Salvation?

I

Since God was conceived of as the embodiment of perfect righteousness and the lawgiver who enunciated what is righteous, and the Devil was conceived of as the embodiment of evil and the one who lured men away from God, it was inevitable that the blessings of the Kingdom of God should have been limited to those whom God could declare righteous, and that the rest of mankind should be regarded as enemies to be defeated and made impotent. Therefore *the Kingdom of God has to become a conquering kingdom.* First Israel and later the Christian church became the army upon whom God depended to accomplish this spiritual world dominion. First the Messiah of the Jews was believed to be the one destined to become the royal representative of God on the earth. Later it was believed that this role would be taken by Jesus who has been regarded by the Christian church as the true Messiah. For Christians Christ became captain and Savior of the redeemed, and they in turn became soldiers of the cross. As has already been pointed out, *the feeling tones of the old Story of Salvation are those of war.* The good life was pictured as a fight against the forces of darkness. Hence the attitudes of the redeemed brotherhood toward those who failed to conform to the Christian pattern were those of condemnation, and their punishment was foretold in the Bible story. The peace achieved through such a kingdom was a peace gained by conquest and separation rather than a peace gained by negotiation and union.

Jesus of Nazareth, who is commonly believed to have been the founder of this Christian religion, probably never conceived of himself as becoming a king or a world ruler. The man who said, "Love your enemies; do good to them that hate you,"[1] does not fit the role of leader of armies, carrying a "blood-red banner" into battle.

Many, even in ancient times, have dreamed of another kind of world brotherhood. And now our generation is yearning with a new hope. Although the outlines of our dream are still hidden in the fog banks of our thinking, yet what we think we foresee both disturbs and fascinates us. We realize we must somehow live together as one world-community without wars, negotiating our differences rather than forcing the weaker party to submit to the stronger. Totalitarianism, in the spiritual as in other realms, is no longer a satisfying concept. Mutual understanding must replace prejudice. Trust in one another's word must replace suspicion. Accenting our common aims must replace exaggerating our differences. Seeing good in our enemies must be substituted for seeing only evil. Honesty must take the place of deceit. Study of the things that make for peace must supersede study of the things that make for war. We must learn ways to encourage people rather than ways to vanquish them. The psychotherapeutic ways now being advocated for dealing with children and adults in the smaller units of family and community need to be applied also to international and interracial relationships.

II

Returning to the old Story of Salvation, let us note that the God of this human drama is presented as *transcendent*, living in a realm beyond human experience, a divinity who rules his subjects by divine command. With such a God, *religion tends to be a matter of external sanctions and obedience to a will other than one's own.* Such a religion means following a way of life which can be known only through some kind of supernatural revelation. Such revelations come to certain divinely appointed messengers through whom the way is known. These "men of God," therefore, in such a kingdom are the persons with power: a hierarchy of authority becomes inevitable, beginning with the Messiah or the Christ, and coming down through popes, cardinals, bishops, priests, and elders, until the common man is reached. Such a general outlook makes religion authoritative, dogmatic and external.

If the God of the old Story of Salvation were an immanent God, such as Walt Whitman believed to be in every face he saw and in every place he walked, such an emphasis on keeping in harmony with God's ways would not detract from the development of one's own inner resources. The original Story of Salvation, however, was not a gospel of "the inner light." It was the story of human control by a power outside and above humanity. George Fox and William Penn must have found their inspiration for "the inner light" directly from Jesus or from their own intuition, in spite of the externalism of the old Story of Salvation.

III

Since, in the Story of Salvation, the lines are sharply drawn between good and evil, the result is not only that the two elements are continually at war, but that *man's choice is between absolutes.* On the one hand is perfection; on the other, despicable wickedness. The one group will be rewarded with eternal bliss; the other will be doomed to complete and everlasting misery. There are no groups in between, no allowance made for immaturity or growth. Absolute principles and perfect ideals — these are the standards by which men will be judged.

This emphasis on perfection has deeply influenced the methods used in the spiritual guidance of children, as well as the preaching role of the church. Either people have been frightened by fear of future punishment, or they have been exhorted to strain after perfect ideals. With the lessening of the emphasis on punishment, there has been a corresponding increase in the accent on idealism. In Christian literature especially, Jesus has become the incarnation of a perfect ideal toward which all should strive, even young children. The question then that needs careful consideration on the part of religious educators is not, Are ideals valuable? but, What kinds of ideals are valuable? And how significant is the process by which an ideal is built? How much does it really matter for good or ill how one feels about his ideals?

Dr. Karen Horney has distinguished between an "authentic ideal" and a neurotic "idealized image."[2] She says that the former encourages and vitalizes development, but that the latter thwarts it; and that the most crucial steps in one direction or the other are usually taken in early childhood. Unfortunately religious groups generally are still quite unaware of the serious psychological problems that are involved in the way ideals are taught. The subject deserves a much fuller consideration than is possible here. A few hints only can be given regarding the new psychological insights.

Authentic ideals, for example, come slowly into consciousness. They grow in the child's ongoing experience, usually developing to the best advantage when there is a minimum of admonition and a maximum of satisfying inter-personal relationships. They come primarily from the child's own emotional dynamics. As the child becomes aware of them, he feels they are truly his own. Such ideals a child can analyze, and criticize; as a result he may change or even entirely discard them without feeling guilty or ashamed.

On the other hand, the ideal that can thwart personality development first comes to the child from outside himself.

It is usually a mature standard, an absolute principle to be practiced or an idealized person to be imitated. It comes with the pressure of an outside authority or with the subtler pressure of the need for love and approval. It tends to become a static ideal to be worshiped rather than a growing ideal that inspires effort. Its function is not so much to guide as it is to approve and condemn. Such an ideal cannot be changed or discarded without inducing feelings of guilt.

Why does such an ideal thwart personality growth? Because, for one reason or another, the ideal does not harmonize with the child's own real or inner ideal and because it is beyond his ability to attain. There is a pathos in the seriousness with which children often strive after the impossible ideals adults expect them to attain; and there is tragedy for the children in the loss of approval and even of love with which they are sometimes threatened when they fail.

Some children, because of their great need for approval, try to hide their failures; they must convince both themselves and others that they are like the ideal that is approved. Others become weighed down by feelings of inadequacy and even of shame; they develop a "despised image" of themselves, and live timidly and ineffectually under the shadow of their shortcomings. Others, being more conscious of the discrepancy between the ideal person they are trying to convince themselves they "should" be and what they secretly know they are like, alternate between their efforts to be the "ideal" and their resistance to it. Still others become definitely negative toward the ideal pressed upon them. These may of necessity conform, but inwardly they will be building up accumulations of resentment and sometimes even of hatred toward all who dictate to them. Later in life they may try to break loose from all external authority, and attempt to live in a false, chaotic independence. Whatever may be the reactions of children who thus feel imposed upon by impossible ideals or by ideals which inwardly they do not desire, all alike will live under unnecessary tensions. Although it is not an easy undertaking to live a life of growing worth, neither should it become so serious and so difficult that it seems impossible.

The neo-orthodox group of Christians, however — if the author understands them correctly — believe that just such severe tensions must be felt and accepted between the absolute and perfect ideals of God and the evil passions which belong by nature within man. They explain that it is man's inevitable "predicament" to be under God's condemnation, and utterly helpless to save himself from destruction. It is only when the tension becomes unbearable, they say, that man will have the needed motive to seek divine forgiveness. Only by the gift of God's grace can he be empowered to hunger and thirst after righteousness with success.

The educational process which such a theology would sanction has been impressively challenged by data gathered from psychiatric clinics. Among those who have found it needful to seek psychiatric advice, large numbers have been people who strained too conscientiously during childhood after the high ideals their parents set for them. This idealism that had been superimposed upon them had created divided desires, and unconscious pretenses contrary to inward realities. Worn and confused by the turmoil of the inner conflicts they had been unable to resolve, they were either trying to flee from the disturbing realities of daily life to find peace, or trying to fight their society in order to gain those normal feelings of personal power they had lost.

Such idealism, therefore, instead of being an aid to spiritual health, blocks the flow of vitality. Indeed there are those who regard such idealism as religion's greatest enemy. In the field of religious education, it has often deceived men into thinking that if ideals are put into words they will also be put into deeds. It has led leaders of children to think that goodness has been taught when Scout creeds have been spoken, Bible verses repeated, or Jesus Christ adored. "Our

Christianity is very sick, and it cannot recover until it is cured of idealism": these are the strong words used by Dr. John Macmurray.[3] One of the tragic ironies of history is that such original and creative geniuses as Buddha and Jesus have been extolled as perfect patterns for all men to emulate. In the very struggle to be like someone else rather than to be one's own true self, or to do one's own best in one's own environment, a child is in danger of losing the pearl that is really beyond price — the integrity of his own soul.

It is not merely the first chapter of Genesis in the old Story of Salvation, then, that needs to be changed to fit a belief to free us to expect and work for greater moral achievements in evolution. Our general practice of looking to the past for the perfect incarnation of all moral values also needs to be abandoned. An evolutionary outlook in ethics, as well as in religion, is needed to keep us attentive to the present, and to free us to expect and to work for greater moral achievements in the years to come.

IV

It is important also to recall the deep note of pessimism regarding human nature that sounds throughout the entire drama. *The only hope of a world-wide kingdom of righteousness lies in God's supernatural intervention.* The Golden Age was in the Garden of Eden, a condition which man might have known continuously, but which he lost because of his sin. The Story of Salvation foretold a progressive deterioration. Seventeenth-century theologians used to write of the Golden Age as having been succeeded by the age of silver, then by the age of bronze and finally by the age of iron. This they thought was the last before the great cataclysm. John Donne in saying "the age is iron and rusty too" expressed the strain of pessimism that pervaded his century. Man was doomed at the outset to an unsuccessful series of crises in the conflicts between good and evil unless he accepted God's offer of salvation — a salvation, however, which does not become fully operative until history is past.

In a period such as ours, when we are constantly reminded of the threat of atom and hydrogen bombs, this theology of unsuccessful crisis is again being preached. The Story of Salvation gives sanction to this position. If, however, such pessimism remains in our concept of human destiny, how can it be absent from our concept of God? Or, if we must believe in God because we cannot believe in ourselves, we are surely in a sorry plight. Humanists and liberals have been accused of being unduly optimistic regarding human capacities; yet, psychologically speaking, clinical experience has shown it wiser to err on the side of self-confidence than to start with a belittling of one's own powers. Had Western civilization accepted a pessimism regarding the human powers of *mind* analogous to the pessimism which the church has tried to implant in men regarding their *moral* capabilities, we would probably be living still in the age of wood fires and candles.

V

Again, *in the old Story of Salvation, the atmosphere is one of special privilege* for those whom God has "chosen" as the subjects of his special guidance and care. Although the goal sought through the extension of God's rule is universal, yet the achievement of this goal is regarded as possible only by the acceptance of Israel as God's intermediary, or by the acceptance of the Christian Savior as the only one through whom salvation may be given. In both cases, one group has the position of power and special privilege. Either the Messiah of Israel or the Christ of the Christian church is to become the King of Kings and Lord of Lords. All other peoples will acknowledge that their gods are not the true gods, and they will bow in humble obedience and adoration before the God of Israel or the God of Christians, who would then be acknowledged as the one true God of all the earth. Even though many other groups would finally accept the terms of salvation voluntarily, yet they could scarcely escape the feeling, as Dr. Max Schoen has pointed out, that "the blessings they enjoyed were not of their own making. . . . The gateway of the kingdom could be opened to the heathen not because of their own merit, but by the grace of Israel, and on terms specified by Israel."[4]

Such a dream of a world kingdom is a dream of benevolence toward those in want. It is a rule of the powerful over the weak. No matter how ethical, kindly and generous the rule may be, it remains a community of superiors and inferiors; for in the warp and woof of its ideology there lingers the belief in God's having played an exclusive role, with a "Chosen People" or with a "Chosen Church" through whom alone salvation can come. The others are denied God's grace except on the terms outlined in the plan.

Such a dream of world relationships, however, falls short of today's dream of universal brotherhood. With the forming of the United Nations where over sixty representatives of different nations, speaking different languages, can sit in one room and speak face to face and be understood, we are both thrilled and embarrassed by the closeness of our contacts. Our common living room is now the whole earth. Whether we will or no, our neighbors are on the other side of the globe as well as next door. In the light of this spaciousness in our exchanges, we find it unseemly to imagine ourselves superior. The realities of our shortcomings are all too easily observed by other nations and groups. Nor can we arrogate to ourselves an exclusive religious revelation. The Scriptures of other religions are easily accessible to every scholar. Any one group today that tries to dominate the whole world by its ideology or by military might, or by force of any kind, will eventually win only the hatred of those who are put under its power. The old methods of showing strength, of using pressures inherent in one's position of power, whether in the family of nations or in the small family of five or six persons, grows less and less effective as the desire for more democratic relationships increases among the peoples of the world.

VI

Finally we note *in the old Story of Salvation that emphasis is primarily on personal salvation, rather than on community salvation.* Personal character is thought of as a prize to be won by each individual through his relationship to God; or it is regarded as a gift of God's grace granted to certain individuals. Meditation on the Law day and night or adoration before the image of the perfect Christ is encouraged. Since the hope of attaining these exalted ideals is postponed until life after death, attention is turned away from the actual human scene, except to awaken the desire to convert as many individuals as possible in the human community before it is too late to obtain God's grace.

This emphasis on the individual in the Christian gospel has been perhaps one of its greatest assets. It has no doubt contributed markedly to our concern for the hungry, the sick, and the afflicted. No one was ever too inhuman or debased to be the object of the tenderness of a St. Francis. "The infinite worth of the individual" is often spoken of as the unique blessing of Christianity. Catholic and Protestant alike declare everyone a potential child of God. None would deny that there has been high value in this emphasis upon the individual. When, however, we claim too much for our virtues, we usually fall into serious error. For this discussion we must note one unfortunate pattern of thought which this emphasis on the individual has fostered — a pattern which hinders rather than advances our progress toward the dream of world brotherhood that lures our generation.

This unfortunate pattern is that *character* has come to be thought of as *something self-contained, achievable singly,* apart from the nature of the society in which the individual

lives. In programs and books planned for character education, attention has commonly been centered on the kind of a
person one ought to be. In Christian circles, the question has
frequently been: What kind of a person should a Christian
be? Then consideration is given to the traits of character
which are to be found in such a person, and stories and discussions are organized around these traits. Children are encouraged to watch for these traits in themselves and others.
They are sometimes asked to bring in examples of honesty,
kindness, and unselfishness. Prizes indeed are sometimes offered for the best examples. The child is asked, as it were,
to accumulate a set of virtues. These virtues necessarily manifest themselves in social situations, but the child gathers the
virtues not for the sake of being useful so much as for the
sake of achieving in himself superiority in character — an
"I-above-you" attitude. Such methods have unduly accented
personal pride and aroused jealousies and hostilities toward
others even while encouraging good deeds.

Although such methods have been largely abandoned in
enlightened nursery and kindergarten education, they still have
much vogue in the work of our religious schools with older
children. We still give children the impression that excellence
of character is something one can achieve alone before God.

Without minimizing in the least the worth of the individual,
we need today to turn children's attention to the "togetherness"
that is involved in worth-while living. Instead of accenting
our independence of others, we need to realize that life never
ceases to be a giving and a receiving. If our long-time goal
is the salvation of a world community rather than merely
the salvation of a few select individuals within this universal
community, our concept of individual responsibility is changed,
and our feeling for our relationship to God is changed. We
no longer feel like racers each rushing to gain his own crown
of glory. Nor do we feel like worthless sinners, begging for
pardon before the Judge of all the earth, hoping to be rescued

from a destruction that threatens most of the rest of mankind. Instead we feel joined together in one family, all seeking for a richness of life never before known. We feel as learners, adventurers, experimenters. With God living in us, we seek together to find out how to bring new values into living, how to widen our feelings of fellowship — not with saints alone, but with all kinds of people.

If our conception of a common goal is thus changed, then our way of guiding children in the direction of this goal will also change. The long-time goal and the short-time daily and hourly goals must be related, else the goal itself will turn into a mirage. Even though we see the possibility and the nature of this universal goal but dimly, yet we can discern some of the immediate steps that are required. At least four of these seem of much greater importance than they have been given in common practice.

1. Both adults and children need to learn new ways of relating themselves emotionally with others. As parents and teachers, we need to learn to give children love rather than discipline. We need to develop the expectancy that we can trust one another, rather than the expectancy that we are going to be taken advantage of, or cheated, or harmed. Adults and children alike need to learn how to connect what is basically good in themselves with what is basically good in others. We shall have to practice making contacts with people, first on the level of our emotional agreements, and from there to rise to consider the divisive elements that hinder our co-operation.

2. It is important that children and youth be led to feel that new discoveries are needed in the realm of religious and ethical living fully as much as in the physical sciences. Since we are dreaming of a goal never before envisioned or achieved, we shall have to develop an exploratory and experimental attitude toward all the problems involved in our living together with healthy satisfactions and peace.

3. Such a dream of an international and interracial community of goodwill can be approximated only by emotionally healthy persons in an emotionally healthy form of society. Our church and synagogue schools should, therefore, regard it as one of their most important functions to lead children in such ways as will encourage their progressive development into emotionally mature people. To this end, the help of psychologists and psychiatrists should be enlisted.

4. Learning how to participate in bringing into actuality the kind of new world brotherhood of which we are dreaming is no simple matter of learning to distinguish between right and wrong. We shall not make much progress merely by enunciating principles or by holding up ideals. The good ways that lead to more abundant living for all mankind are multiple. They will vary under different situations. They will change with our changing outlooks. There are always values on both sides of any conflict. A satisfactory solution when it is worked out must have those values in it in some balanced proportion. Indeed, *learning to balance values rather than seeking to oppose one value against another* is the new art of living we need today.

We must remind ourselves, however, that the hope of a new world brotherhood along democratic lines is not really new. Two thousand years ago, Jesus refused to find satisfaction in the common Jewish hope of a Kingdom of God founded on the subjugation or destruction of the nation's enemies. His vision of a Kingdom of God was not that of his nationalist contemporaries; nor was it the vision later portrayed in the Old Story of Salvation. There is good evidence in the gospels to support the conclusion that Jesus believed that an entirely different kind of world brotherhood not only was possible in this natural world, but even was within the grasp of his own contemporaries. But Jesus' hope of a world brotherhood required tearing down the walls of hate that confined love to those whom it was easy to love. His thought involved learning to love even one's enemies.

Some five hundred years earlier, another of the world's master teachers, Confucius, contrasted the state of disorder, conflict, and corruption prevailing in the China of his day with a time he called the *Ta T'ung* — "the Great Togetherness." This worthy state of things Confucius thought of not only as having once prevailed among the honored ancients, but also as a state that could be restored when men again would live in accord with their true human nature. This "Great Togetherness" would be formed by the universal practicing of the natural human principle of *Jen* — a Chinese character which cannot be translated adequately by one English word. Negatively, *Jen* means eradicating all malice and desire to injure others. Positively, "a man possessing *Jen* extends his consideration for those whom he loves to those whom he does not love." *Jen* means equal sharing, reciprocity, fellow feeling, imaginative identification.

In the *Li Chi*, the ancient Book of Rites, Confucius sketches briefly, with the imaginative skill of a genius, certain conditions that will be common when *Ta T'ung* becomes effective. For twenty-five centuries this picture of hope has been preserved — still as fresh and unlived as a new day dawning:

When Ta T'ung [the Great Togetherness] becomes effective, all men everywhere will live for the common good; leaders of worth and ability will be selected; their words will be trusted and they will be makers of peace. Men will not love their parents to the exclusion of parents of others, nor their own sons to the exclusion of sons of others. They will provide sustenance as long as they live to the aged, employment to the able-bodied, opportunity for development to the young, friendly care to widows, orphans, childless men and the disabled; for each man a task and for each woman a home. Not wishing to be wasteful of their possessions, they will nevertheless not keep them for purely personal use; not wishing to be inactive in the application of their strength, they will at the same time not exert it merely in their own behalf. Thus evil devices will cease or fail to prosper, robbers and traitors will be out of work, and outside doors will not need to be closed. This will be what we call Ta T'ung.[5]

11

The Art of Group Leadership

TO YOU, our children, who hold within you our most
cherished hopes, we the members of the Midcentury White
House Conference on Children and Youth, relying on
your full response, make this pledge:

From your earliest infancy we give you our love, so
that you may grow with trust in yourself and others.

We will recognize your worth as a person and we will
help you to strengthen your sense of belonging.

We will respect your right to be yourself and at the
same time help you to understand the rights of others,
so that you may experience cooperative living. . . .

We will encourage you always to seek the truth.

We will provide you with all opportunities possible to
develop your own faith in God. . . .

— PLEDGE TO CHILDREN, *White House Conference,*
December 7, 1950

NO MATTER HOW ADEQUATE the materials put on the printed
page may be, the intimate and most vital responsibility and
opportunity rests with the group leader. The name "group
leader" is here used in preference to "teacher" in order to
clear away the impression that the function of such a person
is to give instruction, to pass on knowledge, to affirm beliefs,
to preach principles or to proclaim a message. According to
the natural way of guiding child development which has been
suggested in this book, the art of group leadership is conceived
to be an intimate process of mutual discovery and learning.

156

To lead is to give intelligent guidance rather than to promulgate the beliefs of a particular religious society.

Leadership means providing the setting and the warmth of atmosphere that will encourage intelligent and hearty fellowship and a sympathetic outreach of interest.

Leadership means being an imaginative artist, learning ways of awakening interest in new fields of knowledge and experience. It means being creative oneself in one's own thinking, and expecting the same of the children.

Leadership means being well prepared, planning in advance, yet ready to shift gears in response to the children's needs and interests.

Leadership means being well informed and interested in the subject matter to be investigated. It means being able to turn facts stated on the printed page into human experience, to bring written records to life and so to link them with the children's own feelings.

Leadership means being able to respond sensitively to children's moods. It means knowing when to hold a discussion, when to initiate a robust activity and when to encourage quiet thoughtfulness.

Leadership means learning the techniques of group discussion and guidance: what kinds of questions to raise, how to phrase them in order to grant unhampered freedom of expression, how to discover children's interests, how to listen to children's conversation, how to provide order and continuity in discussion without dominating the group's thinking.

Leadership means knowing how to read and tell stories well, how to give variety in tone and speed in accordance with the feeling and thought. Leadership means learning how to live through a story imaginatively and how in telling it to re-create the full experience.

Leadership means learning how to help children to review their experiences through original drama and role-playing, through free art expression and through discussion — choosing the medium on the basis of the group's ability and interest.

Leadership means psychologically sitting on the floor with the children, sharing in the blame for failures as well as in the celebration of achievements. It means being able to laugh with children and also being able to weep with them.

Leadership means growing in one's understanding of children's inner worlds of feeling, their emotional conflicts, their fears, and their special needs for love. Leadership means seeking friendly relationships with children, learning their life histories, recognizing their primary problems at home with their parents and siblings. It means learning how, through personal and group therapy, to help them solve these conflicts without having their spontaneity of emotional expression hampered.

Leadership means learning when to give one's own opinions frankly and when to restrain oneself. It means opening up one's own feelings and thoughts easily and naturally rather than pontifically, expressing one's puzzlings and wonderings as well as one's assurances. It means being able to give one's reasons.

Leadership means learning to enjoy living with children, learning to love oneself and one's opportunities with them. Leadership means learning to love especially the child whose attitudes are the most unlovely of all.

Since seeing and hearing for oneself is more fruitful than merely reading a theoretical presentation of a point of view, let us now pause for the length of a chapter to consider several projects or series of experiences in which children are finding out, thinking, and feeling for themselves, and are growing by means of their own experiencing. We shall briefly recount episodes, taken from the records of church school teachers, which present children of different ages with different needs and problems. It should be noted that in the church schools from which these episodes have been taken, the Sunday morning session was from two and a half to three hours in length.

Max Has a Personal Need

Four-year-old Max, when he first entered the nursery group, refused to play with any of the playthings in which the other children took delight. He would stand at the side of the room apart from the others and merely watch.

The teacher was much puzzled by his extreme aloofness. As she became acquainted with the family she found that Max was the youngest child, and that he had four older brothers, all capable and outgoing. But Max had had six months of illness during which time he had been helpless in bed, separated from contact with children of his own age. During convalescence Max had been obliged even to learn to walk again, and his ability to talk had been greatly retarded. Shortly before his coming to this nursery group the family had moved to the city from a foreign country. The whole environment was strange. Max knew no other young children. He was pitifully dependent on adults for direction.

The teacher was warm and encouraging in her attitude towards Max from the beginning, but he was sober and unresponsive. She noted one day, however, when the group was on the playground, that for long periods at a time Max's eyes would wistfully follow another boy who was riding very expertly on a tricycle with a little red wagon attached to the rear. The teacher, in an effort to encourage Max, lifted him up on the tricycle, put his feet on the pedals, and showed him how to pedal and steer. But Max was afraid: he could do nothing.

This same pattern of behavior was followed morning after morning: the teacher gently encouraging him, but Max always unable to do anything but stand and watch. Several weeks went by, and it seemed to the patient teacher that Max would never learn to play. Finally one morning, to her surprise, on entering the playground he ran at once to the tricycle, mounted it himself, and rode away. His face shone with pride. Presently he got down, found the little red wagon, fastened it to the tricycle, and for forty-five minutes — by the teacher's actual timing — he rode around and around.

This hour of achievement marked a crisis in Max's life. His teacher called it a religious experience although there was no mention of God, and no moral principle was enunciated to the lad. He had not been urged to be courageous. Yet the dark look of timidity was washed from his eyes. His facial expression and all his actions bespoke a new self-confidence. It was as if he had been born again. Soon after that day Max began playing with other playthings. Day by day his speech grew clearer. He even became able to assert his rights against the aggressiveness of the other children. Slowly he grew in resourcefulness and initiative. By the end of the year the teacher called him a happy, reasonable, responsible child, glowing with the normal childlike enthusiasms.[1]

Comment. In how many church or synagogue schools would such a life-giving experience have been possible? Many such schools have few large playthings. Many religious leaders do not realize that a child's toys are his tools for learning how to live with others in kindly co-operation, and that a child learns more through his own experiments than he can ever learn through the admonitions of adults. Furthermore, in many churches and synagogues, the rooms are small, and the schedules for Sunday morning are crowded with other things to do which are regarded as more important than play. Most teachers of religion would not expect that a small child could have a religious experience through achieving the courage to ride a tricycle. Indeed, such an activity would be widely questioned as appropriate for a Sunday morning. It was fortunate for Max that he was introduced to a teacher who recognized his deep need, who could love him in a mature way. In this class a teacher of religion was pioneering in a new way of ministering religiously to a child.

The Birth of a Chick

A group of six-year-old children had been finding out about animals of many kinds, and had heard stories of their being born. One Sunday morning they went to visit a chicken farm. There they not only saw hundreds of chickens, but also visited the incubator room. In some of the drawers the chicks had already been hatched. In others most of the eggs were still unbroken. From one of these drawers the poultry man took out an egg that had a "window" broken through its shell. Kneeling in the center of the circle of children, with the egg in his hand, he showed them the little "window" and explained what was happening. He broke the shell gently, and, as one child said, "he borned the chicken." With absorbed attention the children watched the chick struggle, finally take its first breath of air, and then squirm around until at last it got on its feet and flapped its wings and cried "cheep."

When the chick was put safely back into its warm home, and the door of the incubator was finally closed, the children's emotional release took different forms. Some ran around the room, others clung to the teacher's hand, or began to talk. "I liked to see that chicken born." "It made me feel funny inside." "I didn't know it was like that." "Just think, all these hundreds of eggs are all pecked away with chickens inside." "How does the chicken know how to peck all by itself?" "That was the first time it ever cheeped and we heard it!"[2]

Comment. This moving experience of watching the birth struggle of a small chick was akin to what many a doctor or nurse or father who has watched the birth of a human baby has described as "a deeply religious experience." Both children and adults were aware of something coming forth — new, not made by human mind or hand, like themselves feeling alive, struggling to move on to the next stage of growing. To the degree of their varied abilities they identified themselves with the newborn wonder, and in so doing they felt a reverence for life itself. They sensed its mystery and felt a part of it. Such feeling experiences with other living things develops one's power of empathy — to feel with animals as well as with other human beings. In the birth of a small chick the mystery of life was revealed in a form simple enough for the six-year-old to appreciate.

Which Is the Real God?

A class of eight- and nine-year-olds had been learning about different peoples — the Bushmen of Africa, the Blackfellows of Australia, certain American Indian tribes, the Chinese and Japanese. They not only had read their ancient stories about the beginnings of earth and sky, but they had also found out many other things about these peoples. For example, they had discovered that the Iroquois Indians celebrated their annual Thanksgiving in a five-day festival. As a class, therefore, they had dramatized a part of this festival for a larger group of children, and had written and used in their assembly a litany of Thanksgiving of their own.

Through all these experiences, the children's respect for these other peoples had been expanding. Furthermore, they had been discovering that people have had different names for God, as well as different ways of imagining him and of praying to him.

Finally, one day Richard burst out with the puzzled exclamation: "Well, what bothers me, when we have all these stories about different gods making the world, is — which is the real god?"

Mary quickly said, "Why, our god is the real one, of course — the American god."

"But," asked Richard, "does the American god have anything to do with other gods?"

"No, not a thing," replied Mary. "If the Chinese and all of them pray to their gods they are just wrong, and they ought to know about ours."

"I guess he doesn't pay any attention to the Chinese and those others at all, does he?" asked Ellen.

"But how do we know we just picked out the right one?" queried Richard.

Then the children began to try to figure out just whom they meant by the American god. They became much confused as they thought of foreigners in America. There was a Chinese boy living in the same apartment house as Richard. Was his god an American god?

Finally, with hesitation, Richard tried once more to speak his thoughts. "I believe that the real truth is that there is just one god who started everything. And maybe we don't know about him ourselves. Maybe some of these people were right. But anyway, even if they were praying to the wrong one, I think the right one heard what they all said." He stopped. He seemed embarrassed. "I guess I don't know just what I think. Yes, that's it — but I wish we knew exactly. I wish there was some way of finding out who the real god is."

Nor were these discussions about God carried on for just one or two Sundays. The children went on reading more of the creation stories in *Beginnings of Earth and Sky*,[3] and with each new story questions about God arose in one form or another. Sometimes they wondered what kind of thinking they would be doing if they had never seen a book or heard about God. Some of them even delved deeply into questions most adults never raise. For example, the story from China is about a Creator who began as a dwarf, but as he worked making the world and the sun and the stars he grew bigger and bigger, until he became a giant. Richard wondered, "Is the real God like that? Did God grow bigger and bigger as the world got bigger and bigger? I mean did God grow the way the flowers and other things grow?"

But the idea was too strange for young Richard's mind to hold. He fumbled for a moment. The teacher tried to encourage him to go on. But finally he said, "Of course it's all a lie, because God didn't start small in the first place — he was always big and just the way he is now." We regretted that the hand of tradition already lay so heavily upon Richard's mind that he felt compelled to deny his own momentary and independent insight.

At one time during this ongoing exploration, the departmental supervisor was invited to come to the class to help them answer some of their questions. Mary started the discussion by asking the question which they had so often talked over among themselves. "How are we going to find out who is the real God, and what are we to think about him?"

"Have you visited other countries?" asked John.

"Do you think I might have found out about God by traveling in other countries?" asked the supervisor.

"Yes," said John, "I thought you might have seen some of the statues." Then he was embarrassed. He hadn't really meant to say just that. He realized that statues or idols would merely show what other people thought about God.

"How can we go about finding out about the real God?" asked the supervisor.

Ellen said she thought we might find out by going to a museum. "Museums are full of very old things and probably the men there know about God."

Marylin said: "The story in the Bible sounds real to me. It sounds more real to me than the other stories."

This idea, however, was not convincing to the others, for they realized that different kinds of stories appeal to different kinds of people.

"Why do you think there is only one real God?" asked the supervisor.

"My father says the Bible says there is only one God," said Anna, "and so we know."

"But," said Joyce, "the people of other countries wouldn't agree about the Bible."

Duane struggled to put his reasoning into words. He was feeling after a large conception. "There's the sun and the moon and all the stars in the sky," he said. "They're not moving around every which-way. There seems to be Some One keeping them all in order and keeping them moving in the right directions. It doesn't seem as though there could be a lot of different gods. If there were they might fight and we would never know when the sun would rise or the moon come up." This reasoning seemed satisfying to all.

Then the supervisor tacked on the wall a picture which was entirely covered with a piece of cloth. She said: "You are curious to know what this is a picture of, aren't you? I shall lift this one corner of the cloth. From what you can see, what do you guess the picture is about?"

After several guesses by the children a second corner was lifted; then another corner. The guesses changed and multiplied as the children could see more of the picture. With the lifting of a third corner the children were quite sure what the picture was about. Finally the cloth was lifted entirely from the picture. Then they saw that every guess had been partly right, but that no one, seeing only a small part, could know what the whole picture was.

Then the supervisor drew the analogy between what they had been doing and what we do when we try to think what God is like. "God is something like the whole picture. And the whole picture is something like the whole universe, the earth and sky and every living thing there is. If we could see all, and if we could understand all, we then could know what

God is like. As it is, we are like persons looking at only a small part of a very great picture, trying to find out what it is all about. We wonder if we shall ever know all."

Then Ralph brought the whole discussion back to its practical conclusion by saying: "Each one of us can think about the little bit of God that we do see."[4]

Comment. Not all groups of boys and girls, even under the most skillful encouragement, would care to struggle so long with such philosophical problems. Nor are all teachers able to show such respect as did this teacher, for the children's own crude and straightforward thinking. Nine out of ten church and synagogue schools tell but one story of creation and give the children no opportunity to compare the ideas in that story with those in another. Indeed, in most Sunday school lesson helps the Genesis story of creation is introduced by the statement that it is the greatest story of creation ever written; the reason given is that it is the only story among all the stories of creation told among different peoples that begins with "One God." It is now well known that such a statement is false. Furthermore in such an atmosphere of exclusiveness children are unable to think for themselves.

The experience just related represents an approach to our religious heritage based upon the conviction that children need to know about different religious faiths, that only by becoming broadly intelligent can we develop an appreciation of our kinship with the peoples of all races and times. It is based on the assumption that by learning of the differences, children are compelled to think for themselves. They are also given some basis upon which to do their own thinking. When Richard came to the conclusion that the peoples of different countries prayed to different gods and yet the same God heard them all, he had achieved a breadth of appreciation and a sense of our common humanity that in itself constitutes the vital core of a monotheistic faith. A window had been opened, and the children were looking out toward a far horizon — in the direction of a universal religion.

Do Scientists Pray?

A sixth-grade class of boys and girls had been studying Old Testament leaders, but the interest in these stories was beginning to wane. On this particular Sunday morning the class was very restless. The behavior of the boys had been especially exasperating. The teacher finally said plainly that it seemed to her they were wasting their time by coming to Sunday school. Apparently they felt no real satisfaction in doing as they did and they were hindering those in the class who were eager to work. The boys were glum. Finally one of them burst out saying, "What is religion anyway?"

With good common sense the teacher forgot the bad behavior and threw the question back to the children themselves. To her surprise the boys dropped their hostility and began to talk. "Are there other things you have been wondering about?" asked the teacher. A stream of questions came forth, and the teacher wrote them on the board as rapidly as she could.

"Do scientists pray? Do most of them pray or only a few?"

"Why do they pray?"

"Why do people go to church?"

"Why do they want to go to church?"

"Why do *we* go to church?"

"When we are in the seventh grade and can go to church will we want to go? Why?"

"When do people join the church? What do they do it for?"

"Why do people have a feeling like religion?"

"Some people are afraid of death? Why are they?"

"Is worship the same as religion?"

"May we go to church and see what it is like?"

"Can we study these questions?"

Enthusiasm was high. It was agreed that the following Sunday they would go to a church as a class, and they would also work on these questions.

The following Sunday, when the time came to take up their own questions, these were all on the board where the children could see them. "You have asked some hard questions," the teacher said. "Which shall we take up first?" She waited a moment and then said: "For instance, how are we going to answer a question like this: 'Do scientists pray?' "

"Ask a scientist," several said.

"Do you know any?"

"Sure. There's Einstein and Beebe and Ditmars and Schick and Compton and Thornton Burgess." They made a list of eight scientists. Each member of the class chose one man and composed a letter to him, asking him if he prayed and what he prayed for.

It was an exciting adventure. Would these great men answer? And what would they say?

Several weeks passed before the answers came in. In the meantime the children worked on the problem by themselves. The teacher reminded them of what they already knew, that people had been praying ever since the time when the cavemen lived. But since praying is not easy, people have used different things to help them pray. "Can you think of some of these things men have used?" she asked. "Have they always just said their prayers as we usually do?" The answers came thick and fast. Some of the children had a background of study of various primitive peoples. For the first time the teacher felt the whole group really working together.

They had many suggestions. People have used drums to help them pray, also rattles and prayer wheels; Egyptians wrote prayers on scrolls. (Some of the children had seen prayer scrolls in Jewish homes.) Men have used candles, masks, prayer dances and kites (as among the Chinese). Mohammedans kiss the sacred stone in Mecca. Prayer horns are used in India. The children also mentioned fasting, eggs at Easter in Russian churches, bread and wine in our churches, dreams, sacred numbers, statues, pictures, high places like Mt. Sinai, shrines, sacred animals, cats, cows, torches, fire, water in baptism, rosary beads, crosses and bells.

During the Sundays that followed the children hunted for pictures of these things, and for pictures of special places where people went to pray. They explored *Asia Magazine* and *The National Geographic*.

They also painted pictures of themselves at times and places where they felt like praying. Each told the story of his own picture. These included sitting on a bench in the park thinking over something mean the child himself had done, standing by the seashore looking out over a wide expanse of water, walking through a wheat field and wondering at the beauty of the waving grain growing there, seeing some American Indians on the seashore and talking with them, swimming in a lake, looking out over the hills above a lake, and standing at the top of a slope before skiing down.

Phyllis painted a picture of three hills. "The highest one and the hardest to get to," she explained, "is where the *understanding of religion* is. There is still a cloud around religion and it is not understood yet. The sun still has a cloud over it so that the people cannot see the cross clearly that is behind the cloud. The sun is *religion as a whole*. The people who are climbing are a Crusader, a Catholic priest, a Chinese monk, a Russian peasant, and a little child. They are all trying to reach the hill which is the hardest to get to. They are already to the second, and the third is in sight. But they are in doubt whether they will ever reach it. The cross is beginning to shine through, but there is still a shadow on it."

Finally, about two weeks later, three letters arrived ad-

dressed to three of the children. There was great excitement.
Mickey read his first.

> Dear Master Semenoff:
>   In my mind, prayer can be accomplished in various ways.
> A reverent thought in witnessing some wonder of Nature, some
> beautiful and natural thing, and the realization that I may enjoy
> it or be governed by it, seems to me a prayer of thanksgiving —
> an acknowledgment to the Great Guiding Spirit of the world in
> which we live. I often pray thus, consciously or unconsciously.
>   Sincerely yours,
>   RAYMOND L. DITMARS

There was little said after this reading, but it was evident
that the children were reminded of the day they had painted
pictures of times when they had felt like praying.

The second letter, from Thornton Burgess, emphasized how
scientists could not fail to be impressed by the orderliness of
the universe. He for one, therefore, could not help but believe
there was "a divine intelligence," "a Creator."

"The scientists *do* believe there is a Creator!" exclaimed
James. "Why shouldn't they?" said Harry.

When Phyllis opened her letter from Dr. Einstein, her eyes
shone with amazement and then she laughed. "It's in German!" Since no one in the class could read it, Phyllis left the
room to search for an interpreter. Fortunately she soon found
one and brought him to the classroom. The children listened
almost breathlessly as he slowly put into English Dr. Einstein's
letter.

> Dear Phyllis:
>   I have tried to answer your question as simply as possible.
> Here is my answer.
>   Scientific research work has as a basis the assumption that
> all events, including the activities of people, are determined by
> laws of nature. Therefore, a research worker would hardly be
> inclined to believe that events would be influenced by prayer —
> that is, through an expressed wish to a supernatural being.
>   To be sure, it must be granted that our actual understanding
> of these laws is very fragmentary, so in the last analysis the belief

in the existence of these fundamental laws rests upon a kind of faith. This faith has always been further justified through the achievements of science.

On the other hand, anyone who has seriously studied science is filled with a conviction that a spirit tremendously superior to the human spirit manifests itself in the law-abidingness of the world, before whom we, with our simple powers, must humbly stand back. So, the study of science leads to religious feeling which is certainly to be distinguished from the religiousness of less-informed people.

Friendly greetings to you.

Yours,

A. EINSTEIN[5]

Each Sunday brought at least one new letter until all the eight scientists had been heard from. All of the men were courteous and thoughtful in their replies. Each professed a belief in a higher power. Each said that he prayed, but not in the usual ways. One said he could sometimes pray in church, but the others spoke of finding the experience of prayer most often when feeling in the presence of the mystery or wonder of the natural world.

The children were deeply impressed; but the testimony of the scientists was not enough to satisfy them. The more they thought, the more their questions increased. They asked for an interview with the minister of the church. He met them on a weekday afternoon after school, and for an hour and a half they plied him with such questions as these:

"Just what did the scientists mean by the things they said?"

"If you take away the miracles from Jesus' life and you just have a teacher who said things but didn't do any miracles, do you think that people would believe he is as important as they now think he is?"

"Do you think that when the monks were teaching the Indians about Jesus, if they had not said anything about the miracles of Jesus and had just told the Indians about a great teacher, would the Indians have been converted as quickly as they were?"

"Do you think that if criminals prayed they would stop being criminals?"

"Why do we laugh at other people's religion when our own is just as queer?"

"What is God? Of course I have my own ideas, but I would like to know your opinion."

The minister spoke briefly of the scientists and then began to talk about God, and how he himself tried to think about him. He told of a childhood memory when he thought he had seen God. He said: "I remember the first time I ever saw God — or thought I saw him. I was about four. I was sitting on the back stoop, and I saw the stars in the dark sky for the first time. I was sure I saw both God and Jesus up there in the sky. Each one had a high hat on his head. I ran into the house to tell my mother that I had seen God."

The children chuckled. They began to tell of the ideas they used to have. "I used to think God was shaped like a carrot," said one, but she could not tell how she ever got that idea.

The minister tried to explain the invisibility of God, and compared this with the real invisibility of any person. "You are as invisible as God," he said. "You can also be in several places at the same time." He explained how this could be. Many questions followed this introduction. The children showed no desire to leave until the minister suggested it. The afternoon was an unforgettable one for both the children and the minister.[6]

As a kind of climax to this whole venture the children planned a departmental assembly or service of worship. They chose a panel of five children. The entire department of 100 children shared actively in the discussion. Ruth was leader. She opened the discussion by saying:

"We have been learning a great deal about cave people and their religion, and about the Hebrews and other people, the Indians and Egyptians, but we haven't had a chance to talk much about the way we feel ourselves, *inside of us*. Could we talk today about our own ideas of God? Could you tell us how you feel?"

Another member of the panel followed. "We have our ideas. We know what we think, and then again we are not sure it is true." Since the children in the audience were hesitant the leader of the department suggested that it might be easier to tell how they *used* to think of God, and perhaps also how they feel now.

"I didn't wonder so much about God," someone began, "as I did about where we go after we die. I was told the story of the Last Supper and I imagined that when we die we would all sit around a table with Jesus. Those who had been good would sit on his right side and those who had been bad would sit on his left. After awhile I decided that this was not reasonable. Now I keep wondering what will happen after we die."

There were many who told naive ideas that they once held about God.

"When I was a little girl I used to think God was a great king who sat on a throne up in the sky. He had everything he wanted. Women came around him with baskets of flowers and fruits and he ordered what he wanted. He was very kind."

"I used to think God was a big giant, so big he was twice as big as the whole world. I thought Jesus was like God only just the other way around."

"What do you mean, Barbara?" asked the adult leader.

"Jesus took God's place up in heaven and God took Jesus' place here."

"Mother told me God was with me, and I could not see how he could spread himself all over." It was at this point that Ruth, the leader, tried to explain what the minister had said about our being invisible and in more than one place at a time.

Then came the question, "What is prayer?"

"When I was little," said Brooks, "my mother told me to

pray every night before I went to bed. I thought praying was a job I had to do. Now when I am alone I pray. I just feel like it."

"First when I was little, mother made a prayer for me, and I thought I would have to say just that prayer or it wouldn't do any good. Now I think you don't have to say any one prayer. Prayer is something you feel anywhere."

"But how does praying help?" asked one child. Others tried to tell how they felt praying helped them. "If you pray strong enough, praying gives you courage to go out and work up to that thing."

"My mother doesn't believe in God," said another child. "At night she puts me in bed and opens the window. When she is gone I get up out of bed and kneel down and pray. I sneak it in."

There were other puzzling questions raised.

"I can't imagine God and Jesus both. I don't see how there can be two such good people."

"How much proof have we that there is a God?"

"Did Jesus ever do anything wrong?"

"If Jesus did all the miracles the Bible tells about, why doesn't someone do miracles now?"

The forty-minute period for the service of worship passed all too quickly. More children were wishing to speak. They had thoughts to contribute, questions to ask. The service had reached into depths of religious feeling. A quiet intensity pervaded the meeting. The children had opened up their hearts and had talked with a deep seriousness about the way they "felt inside."

Comment. This unusually successful educational venture was due in no small measure to the teacher's sense of freedom to follow the children's lead. Her supervisor encouraged this freedom, supported her throughout the venture, helped her not to be afraid, led her to realize how outside resources and other people might be called in to stimulate the children's thinking. The teacher planned ways by which the children could sincerely and freely participate throughout the venture. She encouraged them to go on and on as long as the interest was strong. She might have stopped with the reading of all the letters, or with the giving of the play, or with the important two-hour interview with the minister. But instead, the children went on and on until they themselves had planned and led a second original assembly of worship. Thus they brought to pass the most impressive departmental meeting of the whole year when they and the other children discussed not how other people believe, but how they themselves "felt inside."

Such thrilling periods of real education do not often occur in a child's lifetime. Some children miss out entirely on having a chance to share in such experiences. The achieving of such ends in religious education calls not only for skill in the arts of teaching; it calls also for a maturing in our own religious beliefs. It is not only the children who need to grow up in faith; it is we ourselves. If our own religion retains in it unconsciously primitive features of magic, if our own religion is pre-scientific in its general assumptions, if our own beliefs are medieval, if we are still clinging to the faith taught us at our mother's knee or even if we are proud because we are still faithful to the "faith of our fathers," we cannot adequately lead children into the new and mature faith that is appropriate for a new world.

12

What Shall Children Study?

All that quickens sympathetic imagining,
that awakens sensitivity to other's feelings,
all that enriches and enlarges understanding of the world;
all that strengthens courage,
that adds to the love of living;
all that leads to developing skills
needed for democratic participations —
all these put together are the curriculum
through which children learn.

WHAT THEN SHALL CHILDREN STUDY in a school of religion? How should the curriculum of such a school differ from that in the regular day school? What is the justification for a special institution, called a church or synagogue school? What is the subject matter that is most appropriate for children in such specialized schools to know and consider?

As long as the educational process is regarded as primarily propaganda for the particular faith for which a church or synagogue stands, it seems a rather simple matter to answer these questions. Children can then be given such subject matter as will introduce them to their own family or group heritage; and the methods used can be those which have proved most successful in bringing about acceptance, conversion and loyalty. Furthermore, the distinction between secular and religious education can be more clearly made by those who can separate reality into two distinctive categories, the natural and the supernatural, or the material and the spiritual. Since these two attitudes, the one regarding the educative

176

process and the other regarding the nature of religion, have commonly characterized generations of religious leaders, it is natural that the curricula for religious schools in the Western world should have consisted largely of Biblical subject matter, plus knowledge of inherited festival observances, creeds, rituals and church history.

For those, however, who have changed their conception of the educational process from one of indoctrination and acceptance of authority to one of creative discovery, intelligent examination and free decision, the question of appropriate subject matter has grown to large proportions. The problem is made even more complicated by the fact that the inherited beliefs of the separate sects and religions have themselves been impressively challenged. Long-held beliefs about God are being tried by fire in a world-wide melting pot. New cosmologies, new concepts of morality, new assumptions regarding human nature and how it most successfully matures are influencing our present generation. Even a basically different outlook on our long-time goal for human living — the hope for one world where mutual respect and friendly cooperation will prevail — is developing painfully but surely.

In such a generation religious education cannot continue to be what it has been and still remain a constructive force in guiding these great changes. We must accept the fact that when the philosophies of life by which one generation of adults lives are radically changed, it is natural that what we emphasize and what we neglect in our programs of religious education will also change. Even though we may disavow any intention of propagating our own particular beliefs, what we hope for ourselves necessarily influences what we hope for our children.

What then are some of the most significant changes which our new and emerging religious viewpoints call for in our planning what our children shall have opportunity to explore?

I

Perhaps the most difficult of all the changes involved is to accept fully the assumption that *there is no special "religious knowledge"* that can be assigned to a church or synagogue school, while another kind of knowledge is appropriate to the public school. If one fully accepts the thesis that all nature is one and that the spiritual and the material are intermingled and interdependent, if one believes that the Unity and Meaning for all existence is something observable, a fact that can be discerned, or a reality that at least all nature seems to suggest, although none can ever utterly grasp, then the phenomena for study are unlimited. We cannot tell in advance from what areas the most significant suggestions may come. The discoverer needs to range widely and freely into many paths. All life, all existence, is appropriate subject matter for investigation. It is no longer reasonable to say that the most important data can be gathered from some one Scripture, or that books that talk of God or prayer, Jesus or Moses, are religious books while books that acquaint children with baby animals, or fishes, or snails, with water and fire, concrete things in the child's immediate world, are secular. The only appropriate limitations in the curriculum for a school of religion are to be learned from the children's interests and the abilities and the knowledge of the adults who guide them.

If we accept the broad meaning of "religion" or "faith" as presented in Chapter 1, we must realize that as the child goes forth into life, as Walt Whitman has so well said, everything and anything he meets becomes a part of him "for the day, or a certain part of the day, or for many years, or stretching cycles of years." "The early lilacs," "the grass," "the morning-glories," "the phoebe-bird," "the sow's pink litter," "the mire of the pond-side," "the old drunkard," "the friendly boys," "the mother at home," "the father," "the family usages," "the tumbling waves," "shadows," the "clouds," "the sense of what is real," "the doubts of the day-time and of the night-time," "the curious whether and how" — all these become a part of the child.[1]

This then is perhaps the first and primary step we need to take in changing our ideas about the subject matter for study in a school of religion. Anything, anywhere, may be appropriate.

We would, therefore, not try first to find how much there is in the Bible or in our cultural religious past that can be made interesting to children. Our primary question will be: What is there in the children's own experiencing that is of importance to them? What kinds of experiences call forth a special wonder or surprise or challenge their liveliest thinking and questioning? Or which experiences seem to bring them the greatest emotional conflicts? Or on what kinds of occasions do they most need adult guidance? If we must find something distinctive in a special school of religion, we need to learn to look for this elsewhere than in a special kind of religious subject matter that is studied. Instead of helping children on Sunday to think about "religious things," we need to learn how to help children to think about ordinary things until insights and feelings are found which have a religious quality. And what is this religious quality or way of studying?

The religious way is the deep way, the way with a growing perspective and an expanding view. It is the way that dips into the heart of things, into personal feelings, yearnings and hostilities that so often must be buried and despised and left misunderstood. The religious way is the way that sees what physical eyes alone fail to see, the intangibles at the heart of every phenomenon. The religious way is the way that touches universal relationships; that goes high, wide and deep, that expands the feelings of kinship. And if God symbolizes or means these larger relationships, the religious way means finding God; but the word in itself is not too important. It is the enlarged and deepening experiences that bring the growing insights and that create the sustaining ambition "to find life and to find it abundantly" that really count most. *When such a religious quality of exploration is the goal, any subject, any phenomenon, any thing, animate or inanimate, human or animal, may be the starting point.*

II

When religious growth becomes a way of seeing for oneself, of examining one's own experiences, of having direct relations with the universe, and from these experiences building one's philosophy of life, *the focus of interest, from the earliest years and throughout all of one's days of learning, will be the present and the near future.*

This is in contrast to the type of curriculum that finds its focus of concern in the study and preservation of a heritage from the past. Instead of this backward look for codes, doctrines and ideals to which to be loyal, our eyes are on the present and on immediate next steps, with expectation and planning for better things to come. This we need to learn to do without giving up any of the respect and reverence due to men of old, and also without apologizing for our expectation that greater things are in store.

To inspire in children a belief in the worth of their present, day-by-day experiences, through their own discoveries, is an important goal for any educator. One public-school principal who examined the child's book *Growing Bigger*[2] reported that it was one outstanding juvenile he had found that really made the child feel the great worth in his own living and learning.

III

This interest in the present, however, does not mean that the Bible should not be studied in our church or synagogue schools. Nor does it mean that children should always discuss their immediate life situations or live in their own little worlds of thought. It means rather that *the Bible, like all other records of historical experience, should be left to study until children are mature enough to profit by a knowledge of the past.*

It is the purposes for such historical study that must be changed. For example, we can no longer lead children into a study of Biblical history in order to find authority for certain ideals or beliefs. Nor do we desire that our youth should especially reverence those parts of the past that are our peculiar heritage, regardless of their own feelings and thoughts about the worth of this heritage. We would have children feel as free to reject the standards of the past as to accept them. The guidance for present living which we would expect from a study of the Bible would be that kind of guidance that comes when one has an opportunity, and is taught how, to compare alternatives and thus to make one's choices on the basis of a larger perspective. The aim would be to enter understandingly into the experiences of the people of the past, and to learn from their faults and mistakes as well as from their nobleness and courage.

It is for the sake of understanding present problems in order to solve them wisely that youth needs to be aware of the past. Part of the shallowness of some present-day education is due to a neglect of the past. Everything, however, has its history. "There is nothing new under the sun." The emotions that hold men tense against changes in forms of behavior are tethered to ancient standards. All things, all problems have their yesterdays, and to live unaware of these yesterdays is to return to the naïveté of primitive peoples.

History stretches out behind every contemporary problem. For example, the feelings between Jews and Christians have gathered their momentum through two thousand years of accumulation. The terrific emotional struggle between Jews and Arabs over the establishing of a new Israel goes back to the original conquest of Canaan. No one can understand the present tensions who is ignorant of this history. We need to know the history, not in order to exalt one people or one religion established in the past, but in order to be wise in negotiating differences that make for present conflicts.

As was said before, our young people today need to know the old Story of Salvation not because we wish to evangelize the world or hope that this type of traditional Christianity will some day be the world religion. Our young people need to know that ancient interpretation of human destiny because it still lives in our Western life. Many of our emotional compulsions and unexamined convictions have their deep rootage in this theology. Some of the noblest of saints and some of the most significant of reform movements have grown from this theology. A generation hoping to guide the world into better ways must understand men's feelings and convictions and how and why they have grown.

IV

It is not less history then, but more, that is needed in the curriculum of a progressive school of religion. Most adults are tragically ignorant of the history of their own churches, and even more unenlightened regarding the history of other churches and other religions. Each religious group has been far too contented to give information regarding its own historical development and its own outstanding work. Christians long thought that all other faiths were false and the less known about them the better. Such an attitude is an anachronism today.

The larger and longer story of how primitive peoples first came to have religious beliefs and why they tried to pray has been almost entirely neglected. It is a part of the story of man's evolution which has either been unexplored or treated with disdain. Yet it has proven to be fully as interesting to children as the story of how man first learned to hunt or to make boats.

An introduction to this broader story of our universal religious heritage should be given to children at the outset of their historical study or at least during its early stages. Children's own experiences of wonder in the presence of the mystery of birth, their fears of the dark and of dreams, their awe in the face of sickness and death, their inner conflicts between right and wrong, and their feelings of littleness and helplessness before the world's great immensities — primitive man also experienced all these and more. Through a vicarious sharing in such experiences, children come to feel related to these ancient ancestors. They develop a respect for men who, without the help of science or books, found a way to face their fears with courage. We cannot but honor our forebears for their sacrificial experiments with invisible powers in their efforts to better their lives and the lives of their clans. Children should know this story of man's religious strivings, not as portraying a kind of religion to be copied, but as revealing the basic nature of all religion with which they can sympathize because of their own experiences.

Instead then of leading children at the beginning of their historical study through the narrow channel of the Hebrew or Christian tradition exclusively, we would give them a broader outlook on man's quest for life more abundant, and a feeling of being deeply related to the whole human race.

Children of today, no matter to which of the great religious groups they belong, need also to become appreciatively intelligent regarding contemporary peoples whose religions are different. Children of all religious cultures need to have an opportunity to know the life stories, not only of their own religious geniuses, but the stories also of all the world's great religious initiators, Jesus, Buddha, Confucius, Mohammed, Zoroaster, Akhenaten, Moses and others. They need opportunities to understand these men as historical persons as well as to know the myths of divinity that have gathered around them.

Modern youth growing up in our modern world needs to find much more understanding of the world's religious history than has been allowed to any previous generation. To treat the history of man's religious experiences as though it were contained in one sacred book about one religiously superior people is to foster narrowness and intolerance at a time when breadth of appreciations is sorely needed. Indeed, the values in one's own religious heritage can never be understood or fairly appraised until one is able to compare his own with others.

V

If we accept an exploratory way for coming by one's general beliefs about the natural world, *we must accept this same exploratory way for discovering satisfying human relationships.* Hitherto, ethical teachings in our Western world have been largely directed toward the achievement of "Christian" or ideal traits of character, and these have usually been found illustrated in Jesus or other great men of the past. We have been accustomed to put the accent on the worth of the individual rather than the group. We have been told we must become moral in spite of an immoral society, as if this were really possible. Through this emphasis on personal attainment of ideals we have accented personal pride, and introduced the need to be superior even in our goodness. Such ambitions have tended to arouse jealousies and hostilities, or an "I-above-you" attitude.

As the science of sociology has progressed, it has been clearly shown that none can be good in isolation. A good life is by necessity co-operative. Dr. Alfred Adler put the matter this way: "When we speak of virtue we mean that a person plays his part; when we speak of vice, we mean that he interferes with co-operation. . . . The individual's proper development can only progress if he lives and strives as a part of the whole."[3]

This does not mean, of course, that we never think of ourselves apart from others, or that we do not develop certain habits and character traits peculiarly our own. There is a degree of originality and uniqueness in everyone. It does mean, however, that the richer our personalities become, the more complex are the ties that bind us to others. Although we should each still seek for personal righteousness, yet there is a false striving for individual values which leads to lonesomeness and fear. To avoid this tendency to find satisfactions in isolation, we would be cautious about making children self-conscious regarding the character traits they are developing, and instead we would turn their attention toward group needs and co-operative endeavors. In short, our schools of religion need to become laboratories where experiments in human relations can be continually developed and appraised.

Even the young child of two, whose society is his family and a few people in his direct neighborhood, has to begin to learn the techniques of interaction with others by which to gain his needed gratifications and by which to maintain warm feelings between himself and others. It is not character traits such as kindness and honesty that he needs to be helped to develop. A child companioned by adults who are permissive and understanding of his personal feelings and needs will naturally, though slowly, discover that other people also have feelings and needs. To learn the "science of human relationships" is to learn the balance between giving and receiving. Living together is much like being on a seesaw. Each one needs his chance to be up as well as down. Both may be valuable experiences. But rhythm between the two is what brings the thrill.

VI

As children's social outlook expands we would give them opportunities to understand the larger strategic emotional conflicts of our time, and through supervised and examined practice we would help them to learn the new techniques needed for resolving large social conflicts.

Every generation has its growing points. These are the emotionally tender spots where new ideas and new needs are emerging, and where the most significant changes are taking place. These sensitive points must not be by-passed as too dangerous for young people to consider, for it is on these issues that new learning is most needed. The growing points of our present world society are different from those in the world's life when the events of the Bible took place. The old technique of fighting over issues is now too catastrophic to hold any promise of good.

But learning how to substitute something more effective than fighting involves more than to accept in principle the Golden Rule, or to follow the teachings of Jesus about loving one's enemies. To find substitutes for war involves more than courageous condemnation of wrongdoing and the proclaiming of ideals. To find the successful techniques leading toward a world of mutual goodwill requires a widespread understanding of human emotional needs. It involves an immense degree of knowledge, a willingness to admit mutual mistakes, and a readiness to learn and follow new techniques that give promise of better things.

Religious education has never before had so serious a challenge to teach new ways in human relationships. To open up such burning contemporary issues inevitably involves danger: to evade them will invite disaster.

VII

Although it is surely of great importance that children should study the problems involved in human relationships, the philosophy of religion which we have here outlined leads us to *put value also on exploring the natural world that lives and moves quite apart from humanity.* To build religious faith on the basis of human relationships alone is narrowing.

Man's feelings toward the natural world of things and non-human beings and his ideas about these have long been linked with religion, and they still should be.

The bane of much religious instruction is its constant use of abstractions, its emphasis upon moral principles, and its wordiness about God. Children and even adolescent youth live most vividly with concrete things. The unseen must be discovered through the seen, and the intangible is first felt through knowing what can be touched and handled. Our religious education needs to be linked much more richly with learning about things, living and non-living, than it has ever been.

Some of the most religiously rewarding children's group experiences we have known have come by way of their discovering the real nature of certain things — having contacts with baby animals, birds, ants, spiders, wasps, and finding out about stones. A group of nine-year-olds carried on several months' study of *water*. They looked at the varied forms water can take; they found out how important it is to all life. They recalled their own delightful experiences with water, and they remembered the times when they had prayed for the rain to stop. They asked themselves what grounds they thought they had for expecting such prayers to be answered. How was rain made? They learned of experiments men had made and how they had produced rain. The children set up a small experiment of their own in rain making. They heard stories from a number of different countries telling of the different ways people have prayed for rain. They found that both the Hebrews of Bible times and even some ministers in our churches today say prayers for rain. They studied about floods and hurricanes, and compared the Bible story of the great flood with another story from the Northwest Coast Indians. They learned why in India people bathe in the Ganges, why our Nordic ancestors hung gifts on trees beside springs, and why today we baptize with water. The class began with this everyday thing, *water,* and from there they journeyed on and on into different countries and into the long ago, and back again to their own feelings, their own prayers, their own thoughts of God, and their own ideas of goodness.

We have known other children to have had equally rewarding experiences while working on units designated as Fire, the Sun, the Wind and Animals. In each case, the children not only learned the scientific facts regarding these things, which present-day science has made evident, but also searched to find out how men in ages past *had felt about these phenomena,* and what connection these things have had with religious beliefs and prayers. That men have felt like worshiping the sun was not difficult for the children to imagine when they once began to think of our complete dependence upon it. The children were surprised to find how important fire still is to the followers of Zoroaster. They had not supposed that so many different kinds of animals had been regarded as sacred. The children began to recognize that animals have powers that man is jealous to have for himself. And it was a new idea for them that our word "spirit" means "breath" — the wind that comes in and out of our mouths; and that the Mayas once called their greatest god Hurakan.

By entering thus imaginatively into the experiences of people in different countries and times and through discussing their own feelings, the children came to feel an emotional tie binding them to unnumbered peoples. Such an awareness of relatedness when it is warm with sympathy and understanding, in spite of differences in knowledge and racial background, comes to have a richness of quality that well deserves being called religious.

But what has all this to do with an ethical religion? The glory of the Christian and Jewish religions is their emphasis on the ethical life. If a child finds God in these common, material things, will he not end by finding only the pagan god of nature? Or perhaps in this scientific age he will find no God at all.

These are pertinent questions as long as one believes that the natural and the spiritual can be separated. As long as we think of moral men living in an immoral natural world, we will try to escape from worldly things. Or if we assume that the universe is neutral or indifferent, we may think that any study of nature is irrelevant in building up a religion, that it may even be a hindrance. The position we take here is that there is no way of escaping nature. If God is God of the human world, he must be God of nature too. And in any case, children should be given the opportunity to explore nature and to come to their own conclusions. Our second reason for dealing directly and profoundly with non-human things is ethical. We have a responsibility to things as well as to people.

1. We have a need to understand our world as far as we reasonably can. "No man can do right in the midst of things he misunderstands."[4]

2. We owe nature our respect. The earth is our Mother. We are the fruit of nature's age-long struggle toward a better world. It is all very well for us to sing our praises and to bring our offerings to God for the bounties of the earth, but we need to do more. We need to show our respect by our practical treatment of nature. Our very existence is dependent on things. Our bodies are made of the same materials as the dust and the stars. If we respect ourselves we also respect the matter through which we live and move and have our being.

3. Nature asks us to assist her in her evolutionary experiment, which was begun before we entered the world, and will continue after our little selves are gone. Nature asks us to help her toward excellence. She does not ask us to be content with things as they are. She challenges us to be co-creators with her, to help her improve on the past. Nature asks man

to put greater value into things. "By doing so he will put greater value into himself and into other persons."[5]

4. Indeed, we cannot have any kind of relationship with other persons without dealing with things. Animals, plants and inorganic substances cannot make a heaven or earth, but neither can man make a heaven here without co-operating with things. All our difficult problems of international ethics are interwoven with our use of things — the world's lands, seas, oil, waterways, air, electricity, minerals, coal, iron, aluminum, copper, uranium. The cultivation and distribution of the foods that come from the earth — wheat, rice, sugar, corn — all these things involve questions of fraud, the "squeeze," excess profits, monopoly versus honesty, co-operation and equalization of wealth.

5. It is not so much that our generation has been too materialistic, that we have valued material things too highly; it is rather that we have sought to have those material values for ourselves at the expense of others. We have not realized that everybody needs these things if we need them. Nor have we planned how all might have them. Instead, we have made material things a symbol of superiority, a sign of belonging in a higher caste. Because of this exclusiveness, our very gains have been turned into losses. Every material thing we use involves some human relationship, and there is always the possibility of a good and a less-good value.

VIII

We would make self-understanding an important and continuous goal in religious development to the end that the child's emotional autonomy may be developed, even though the pressures upon him from society or from authoritarian religion may increase.

Even nursery and kindergarten children should learn to guide their own behavior through beginnings in an understanding of their feelings and needs, rather than because of precepts taught them. Self-understanding is intertwined with understanding others. Children find their own problems mirrored in the problems of others. Consequently the most vital growth in self-understanding may often take place in group experiences. Many teachers and parents are doing much better than they realize by their permissive and democratic ways of dealing with children. Sometimes the best opportunities for learning come when children in a home or a classroom find themselves in a tangle of fevered interests, and must stop to talk the whole situation over in an attempt to understand one another's feelings.

Experimentation needs to be done with units on self-understanding, both with children during the early school years and with older boys and girls. Storybooks portraying common types of conflict situations need to be made available in order that children may project their personal problems on to storybook characters, and through role-playing bring their own emotions into expression where they can be talked over.

The records made in child welfare clinics are filled with stories of burdened, thwarted and deprived children who have been misunderstood and gotten into trouble with society. Some of these might well be rewritten and used as concrete illustrations to help other boys and girls toward deeper self-understanding. Stories from the childhood of great men and women might be similarly used. Reports also from other cultures, describing types of social demands and family relationships other than those we are accustomed to assume as the only patterns, might awaken fresh thinking. Sometimes these matters, which are so intimately a part of our assumptions that we do not think to question their validity, can best be brought into awareness by using contrasting and faraway situations. Some material, including legends and folk tales from the bibles of the world, may be used to start fires of interest or to release frank expressions of personal feelings.

This understanding of the self leads naturally into a consideration of the three great crises in any single life — birth, sexual mating, and death. These universal emotional experiences have always been of importance religiously. Beliefs, myths and ceremonies of many different types have gathered around these three crises. They should be important subjects for consideration at various age levels during the process of spiritual education.

IX

We would, therefore, give the very young child opportunities to sense the mystery of birth through his own direct experiences with animals and babies, and through watching the growth of plants from seeds. In these experiences the wonder of life is dramatized for him. Instead of first presenting the child with the story of the miraculous birth of one outstanding person, such as Jesus, it would seem more natural to deal openly and reverently with the mystery of which the child himself is a part — his own birth and the birth of other living things he can see and know.

It is not only the young child, however, who feels this challenge in the phenomenon of birth. Questions about babies and how they come lie buried in every child's mind. Misconceptions poison many an adolescent's attitude toward his girl friend. Watching the birth of kittens or of a calf, or the hatching of a chick will enthrall any group — young, middle-aged, or old.

The annual observance of the birthdays of Jesus and Buddha, and the birthdays of other great sons of men is evidence of a universal sensitiveness to the mystery in the birth of any personality. It is not the miracles, which are alleged to have accompanied these famous births, however, that keep these festivals alive. It is rather the undying wonder that human beings feel in the presence of a newborn child. It is the miracle of the birth of all children that we should celebrate each year. Our church school programs should expose children to this universal experience of wonder. For example, in one Christmas celebration the children enacted birth ceremonies or scenes from different lands, representing how parents feel and act toward their newborn babies the world around. Again in another school, the high school students enacted, in pantomime and with readers, the miracle stories of the births of Buddha, of Confucius, and of Jesus in succession.[6] The children's appreciation of the poetic and emotional meanings in their own special Christian story was deepened through this experience, and yet none of the three stories could be believed literally. In such experiences children become peculiarly conscious of feelings too deep for words, and thus they come to understand how religious symbols and ceremonies have arisen to express these universal emotions.

X

Linked closely with the mystery of birth is the *mystery of sexual mating*. This second major experience, that of the love of "a man for a maid," throughout all the ages of recorded human experience has been a source of religious feeling. Our religious institutions sanctify marriage with their rituals and blessing. The experience of sexual ecstasy has been thought of both as uplifting and as degrading religion. The feelings of mankind have been violent and contradictory regarding this engrossing life experience. Our schools of religion are the most appropriate places for opening up thought on the problems of mating and marriage and earlier sex education. Instead of avoiding the subject in our curricula we need to meet children's questions frankly, and to accept and respect the emotions involved.

XI

Finally, the third *great crisis of life is death*. Children have contact with death at a very early age. It is an even more startling challenge to thought and feeling than is the experience of birth. Thoughts of death are much more common in children's minds than most adults imagine. Death pervades their play, their dreams, and their storybooks.

Experiences with death have universally awakened religious feelings. Death may have been the first great challenge in human experience to bring man to think seriously of his life and its possibilities. The tragedy of the old Story of Salvation is basically the tragedy of death. Salvation is salvation from death. We have in our Christian and Jewish heritage a thought regarding death which calls for revision. Children need to be exposed to other ways of thinking about death than as a punishment for sin.

"If a man die shall he live again?" is a question mankind is always asking. In our plans for guiding children spiritually we need to give more open consideration to the experience of death, and to the different ways men have had of contemplating it. The volume *Beginnings of Life and Death*[7] gives several myths and thoughts about death. Children who have read these myths about death have been especially intrigued by the story from the primitive Miwok tribe of California Indians, in which death is accepted as being natural and unavoidable if babies are to be born and have their opportunity to live. The story of Adam and Eve and the coming of death as a punishment has never been convincing to the children we have known. One of the thrilling results of opening the doors wide to truth from any quarter is that we are so often surprised.

In one fifth-grade class the interest in the problem of what happens after we die was so keen that the children invited a succession of friends to come to their class and tell them frankly how they thought and felt about death. Another class, who had been studying the story of Akhenaten[8] and had learned how important thoughts of life after death were to the ancient Egyptians, created their own individual dances to express their own feelings about life after death. Death is not a subject to avoid or to evade. Children need to find ways to accept death as well as life. It should be a subject for discussion, dancing, painting and acting, whenever the situation calls for curiosity or concern. The need will come at different age levels for different groups, and teachers of all ages should be prepared to open up the subject. To an older adolescent or college group death is very close in these days of wars and rumors of war. What are the things worth dying for? When is taking the life of another justifiable?

Our world needs some fresh and courageous and poetically sensitive adventuring in this area. Our funeral rituals are antiquated. Young people might well examine them. Creators of new traditions will arise if we free our youth and encourage their original approach. To put truer meaning into death will bring a truer understanding of life.

XI

If, then, this general outline of some of the possible fields for exploration appropriate in a school of religion represents significant changes, it is clear that as religious organizations and as individual leaders we have much to learn and much to achieve.

At present such plans as these for today's children are seriously crippled by the usual church school schedules and environments. This new type of school of religion calls for adventurous planning. It needs better housing in large and pleasant rooms. The furniture should be adapted to the children's needs. The classes should be graded according to the mental age of the children. For the small children there should be plenty of playthings. Big and little students should be able to paint, to make properties for plays, to dramatize their experiences and the stories they read. There should be space for exhibit tables. A library of readable books should be available.

The period for the sessions of the school should be lengthened to at least two hours a week, and preferably to three hours. The children need time to do the things they enjoy. They need time to plan their work together and to negotiate their emotional conflicts when they arise. They need leisure for quiet and leisure for activity. In short, they need time to practice democratic living. Assemblies for worship, to be impressive, must not be hurried. With story or talk, prayer or music, poetry or thoughtful meditation, hearts may be stirred, horizons broadened and high purposes born.

Teachers who can carry through such a type of creative exploration are as yet small in number; and fewer yet are the superintendents, directors of religious education, ministers and rabbis who are even interested in supervising such an undertaking.

The church's resistance to change in its programs of religious education has been persistent and powerful. In the beginning, Sunday school classes for children were started, not by the ministers of the churches, but by small groups of untrained laymen and laywomen who saw an unmet need, and determined to try to meet it. Unfortunately, even to this day, this whole department of the work of the Protestant churches of the world has been left largely to the efforts of untrained men and women. In most of our theological seminaries, education in this field is not yet regarded as demanding the same quality of discipline and scholarship as is thought to be needed for the minister's function of preaching to adults. The prestige accorded the minister to children is low. The courses made available are meager. This lack of a sense of responsibility on the part of ecclesiastical leaders of our denominations and this lack in the education given our ministers in the field of ministering to children have long been and continue to be the most serious drag on the process of change in our church's life.

To learn to participate wisely in the religious development

of children, however, is to learn a profession. It demands scholarship of a high quality in a wide range of fields of knowledge — science, philosophy, history of religions, the Bible and other sacred scriptures, individual and group psychology, education, sociology and world problems. I recall a personal experience when teaching a fourth-grade group of Sunday school children. The director, noting in my report the number of books on anthropology and primitive religion which I had read in preparation, remarked, "I never supposed before that a person needed to know so much to teach fourth-grade children." Of course, the fact was I didn't know half enough. The important changes needed in our patterns of child guidance in religion will not come until we ourselves know more thoroughly and until this demand for scholarship is recognized by our seminaries and by our churches. Nothing superficial or easy will meet the present need.

A new churchmanship is called for if the religious education for today's children is to be vital. *We need new schedules and new equipment, new plans for the education of leaders and parents, as well as a new point of view and a new curriculum.*

13

How About Worshiping Together?

> The mysterious is the very heart of this natural existence
> of which we are a part. It is in every conscious moment.
> It lies buried in the depths of the age-long flow of the "un-
> conscious" of which each small life picks up, as it were,
> but a few drops. The mysterious pervades both life and
> death. No one knows the simplest thing unless he also
> feels there is more that has not been explained. There is
> always a beyond from where we have gone.

BECAUSE OF THE VERY NATURE and significance of religion,
religious growth is an emotional experience as well as an
intellectual one. Church leaders have always recognized the
importance of touching children's emotions. Unfortunately,
some have cultivated the art of influencing children emotionally, but have taken small pains to understand them emotionally. Some have exploited children's emotions in evange-
listic crusades, overwhelming them with ideas beyond their
power to evaluate, and trying to arouse fear or exaggerated
feelings of guilt. Sometimes a moral censorship has been
set up to control the kinds of emotions children are permitted
to express.

Other religious leaders, having become aware of the dangers
involved in such unfair emotional pressures, have conscientiously tried to avoid all appeal to children's emotions in their
work. Liberals have justly prided themselves on the degree
of objectivity with which they could maintain their beliefs
and talk about them with children. This attitude has in its
turn led to the reputation that liberal churches are cold — a
criticism justified more often than we would like to admit.

We are blind, however, if we pride ourselves on being un-emotional in our religious experiences and in our group gatherings. The very task of achieving a reasonable and ex-panding faith must be motivated by deep feelings of need and trust in the universe and by profound feelings of self-respect if the effort is to be sustained. To be granted the opportunity to have one's faith mature in intellectual and emotional freedom is something to be enthusiastic about. The present upsurge of concern among liberals about services of worship, and the apparent yearning for more ritualistic forms, are an expression of this realization that we all not only need to be convinced, but also want to have our feelings warmed.

For generations of adults a service of worship once a week has been the outstanding feature of the church's program. This Sunday morning service has been the one uniting emo-tional experience which has kept congregations of adults loyal. "In these church services," Dr. Angus MacLean writes, "we measure ourselves against the best we know." It is "the only place where we go to acknowledge privately and publicly that we need to be wiser and better people, the only fellow-ship we join specifically to get what I can not describe better than as a God's eye view of ourselves."[1]

If such services have been so significant for adults, can they not have a similar value for children, provided some adaptations are made to children's immaturity? This is the question and the hope that have led to special services of wor-ship for children. In some churches the development of a Junior Church has been the answer. Patterned after the adult church, this service is for children ranging in age from seven or eight years through fifteen, with the older children serving as deacons, ushers, and sometimes as the leaders. As a result of this Junior Church movement, there has been an interesting development of beautiful chapels for children, and of care-fully trained and gowned children's choirs. Great emphasis has been put on dignity, formality, good music and beautiful surroundings. Through these carefully planned services, children's feelings of reverence for God and the church have been enhanced. They have liked being accepted in a fellowship that respects them and gives them their own special opportunities to act as grownups. Their enjoyment is increased also by the pageantry of form and color. In such a setting the leader (frequently the minister himself) gives a message. He becomes the teacher as well as the minister. This in itself adds to the children's feelings of personal value.

This growing interest in services of worship for children is significant. Such children's meetings make clear to children and adults that there is something distinctive in a church school which is not found in a public or a weekday school. As our present communities are set up, in view of the separation of church and state, the children need to feel some such distinction in order to motivate going one day a week to a different place from "the school." Furthermore, experience has shown that children's meetings sometimes have been the most deeply enjoyed part of the entire morning's session, the most unforgettable, and the most enduring in their influence. They have added a depth and a range of meaning to experiences that otherwise might have been trivial. If services of worship can perform such a function they are needed. Religiously significant activities should not be trivial.

If then we believe that some kind of services of worship should be a part of our program in a school of religion, how do our changed religious beliefs and our changed philosophies of education affect the nature of these meetings? Is the usual adult type of "service" a good model for children's meetings? What kind of worshiping does a natural approach to religion call for?

I

Leaders in a growing number of liberal churches are becoming aware of *a dichotomy between the services of worship and the classroom work. They see two philosophies of edu-*

cation represented. The one is the philosophy of leadership by direction and preaching. Words of Scripture are read to emphasize "eternal verities." The leader chooses some great theme or "truth," which he explains and impresses by means of a story or an appeal. The children's participation is mostly passive or takes the form of certain stereotyped duties such as ushering, taking up the offering, or reading assigned passages of Scripture.

In the school part of the church program, however, the children are actively searching to find a basis for a growing faith. They are examining different points of view. Instead of affirming truths, the leaders encourage questioning, experimenting, role-playing, dramatizing, identifying with the feelings of other people. Even doubting is sometimes purposely encouraged in order to deepen thoughtfulness.

Again, in many of our children's services of worship, artistic expression in music, in Bible readings and in prayers is regarded as more important than the understanding of the ideas in these forms. Children are led to repeat words and to sing songs without thinking about them. Indeed, often they cannot think about the words because they do not understand their meaning. This unthinking use of words has been justified on several grounds. It is said: children will some day grow to appreciate the meaning of the words; they are Scriptural classics; children should know them to be educated; the words will comfort them some day when they are old; the words have a majestic sound; the rhythm in them is strong and beautiful. Merely saying the words in unison or in choral speaking is thought to awaken feelings of reverence for the holy, or feelings of divine support.

Making everything understandable to all those participating in a service of worship is said to be an impossible ideal. This is markedly true when children of a wide range in ages are gathered in one meeting. To use words appropriate for six-year-olds that will be challenging at the same time to fifteen-year-olds is quite impossible. We are tempted, therefore, to justify using words beyond children's mental grasp in order to support the traditional service.

In other parts of the church program, however, teachers are making persistent efforts to adjust curricula and activities to the children's natural schedules of development, believing that only thus can they encourage wholesome growth. Words without meaning would never hold the interest of the children in our classrooms, where they are not restrained by the awesomeness of rituals and the quiet beauty of chapels. Besides, we are not preparing children to meet life's difficulties in years to come. We are educating children for the sake of their present living. We wish to enrich their immediate experiences, to help them solve, with emotional sincerity and with intelligence, their present problems. We purpose to help children to live now, with all the resources their hearts and minds can muster, knowing that by so doing we are preparing them most surely to be creative and useful participants in an unknown future.

II

Beside a contrast in educational philosophy there is often *a contrast in theologies*. Some leaders are more sensitive to this difference than others, and it is more marked in some situations than in others. Although the natural approach to the development of religious living does not require uniformity in beliefs among those who are searching together, yet there are certain conceptions of deity and certain attitudes toward prayer which cannot long survive the process of open-minded examination.

Elements of the theology of the old Story of Salvation meet us in our liturgies, Scripture readings and hymns at almost every turn. Even though as liberals many of us have freed ourselves intellectually from much in the old tradition, yet we remain tied to the "faith of our fathers" emotionally. We love the great poetry and music and imagery preserved in our heritage. We insist on singing the Christmas carols and on hearing the story of Christmas over and over, even though the patterns of thought contained in them no longer have rich meaning for us. We could, if we cared to do so, put our thoughts and feelings about Jesus into new symbols that would more truly say what we feel. But the words of the old hymns, old prayers and Scripture passages have become a part of us. It is like pulling up our emotional roots to discard them or even to change a few words here and there. Indeed, if we were honest with ourselves perhaps we would rather not even try to think clearly about their meanings lest something important to us might be destroyed. We feel the need to sustain the emotional uplift which we gain from these forms.

Nor is it difficult to justify clinging to these ancient symbols of divinity because they probably correspond in some measure to reality and truth. The nature of God cannot be expressed adequately by any one type of symbol. If God is everywhere, is he not in the starry heavens as well as on the earth and in the life of man? Sometimes the eyes of God do seem black and stern and terrifying. Sometimes they seem to shine with love or pity. The old pictures of God as Almighty King, surrounded by singing angels, dwelling in a glorious ethereal heaven, with humanity bringing gifts, bowing down, beseeching special help, special protection, special guidance, as gifts of God's good graces — all these symbolic pictures represent feelings widely experienced. If then these symbols have so much of true human experience in them and seem so valuable even to liberal adults, why can we not expect that they will be of value to children also? It is indeed difficult to decide how deep to dig in order to supplant the old symbols with something new. Is it really important to be so concerned?

III

It is our thought that what is devitalizing in perpetuating these old religious symbols, without re-examination, is not that the old are used, but that they are used so unthinkingly and so exclusively. In learning how to lead services of worship that could harmonize with the general philosophy of exploration presented in this book, we have found it needful to learn how to *put into such services the same feelings of wistful wondering and questioning that we sought to develop through the other types of activity in our class programs,* without leaving the children with feelings of insecurity.

Surely the feelings that are awakened when words are used without being thought about or without being understood can be only misplaced or superficial feelings. We know also that children who half understand are in danger of gaining misinterpretations of great ideas. We cannot afford to take such risks.

How can the appropriate feelings of wonder and thoughtfulness be stirred when one pattern of ideas alone is presented as the way to believe? The tendency of the child to follow adult leadership is so strong that if certain thoughts are simply assumed as true, they are likely to be taken over without question. If we wish to have children wondering about God, or the nature of the world in which they live, or if we wish them to think seriously over the problems they must face and resolve, *we must present or open up to them some alternatives.* Children, for example, need to be helped to understand why people have thought of God as almighty king and as living in the sky. They need to understand also why others have thought of God as spirit, or intelligence, or power, or mystery in the here and now, within all things everywhere. They need to learn also why others do not care to think of God at all or to use the word. Nor can we be true to our philosophy of exploration if we end all such questionings with the assumption that Christ knew God as no one else has ever done or can do, that he has shown the truth to all mankind or that in the Bible is the supreme revelation. We need to learn the art of arousing questioning and feelings of wonder without, on the one hand, belittling what our traditions have expressed, and without, on the other hand, being dogmatic regarding the final truth.

IV

We *have found it needful, therefore, to learn how to encourage children to think on the thoughts in their hymns and readings.* Sometimes we have presented an old hymn as expressing one person's way of imagining God and perhaps have added a story about the hymn writer to illustrate why he felt as he did. Sometimes the song has been presented as giving one man's answer to the question we had all been wondering about.

The creation of suitable new songs is sorely needed — songs that children who are being nurtured in freedom of thought and in this natural approach to religion can sing wholeheartedly. A few promising steps are being taken. Several new children's hymn books have recently appeared that indicate real progress.[2] A number of leaders have been searching widely for singable poetry. Some have been experimenting in their own churches with their own carefully selected collections. But the growth of new art forms is naturally slow.

We call hopefully for poets and writers to come forth and give our children songs that they can sing with wholeness of heart. If a new theology is taking shape, if we are living with new understandings of good and evil, if we are striving for a new kind of world brotherhood, we need new songs to invigorate us. We need writers who can become as children in their sensitivities, who can express for them their longings and their wistfulness, and who can give wings to their enthusiasms. It is not easy to say great things simply, but we need the help of those who can learn to do just this.

V

In giving talks or in leading children to participate in discussions the same general principle applies. *Instead of making a pronouncement regarding God or immortality, we start out with some experience and the natural question arising from it.* It has often been surprising to find children under twelve so interested in raising basic questions and so persistent in struggling for clarity, even when dealing with such great philosophical questions as God, prayer and immortality.

Children can be helped when thinking on such large ideas if they can express themselves in other ways than merely in words. One group of ten-year-olds, for example, danced their feelings about life after death, and another class painted their own symbols of God. The variety of ideas they put into their paintings was surprising and indicative of sincere and original feelings. Some represented God as a person, others used merely an eye or a hand, while others used the sun and its beams or merely a nebulous light. The most surprising one of the paintings was one that represented God as a broad beam of color, slanting down from the top left to the lower right of the paper. The center of the beam was red. Beside it on one side was a beam of yellow and on the other a beam of black. "These show," said Merylyn, "that God is part 'bad' and part 'good.' He has to be, if he is everything." We were pleased that she was not afraid to present such a thought. The children had previously heard the Chinese story of creation and had learned how their ancient sages had thought of God as being both the *Yang* and the *Ying*. Merylyn was working on this idea; but she made her own symbol and she used the traditional Western words for the two phases of reality.

Later these children showed their paintings to the larger worshiping group, and one by one they told what they were trying to say through their pictures. This was really an exciting occasion — in a kind of quiet, bubbling way. At another

time the leader showed on a screen, by means of a reflecto-
scope, pictures of a dozen and more different symbols that had
helped different peoples to think of divinity. These included
such symbols as the praying mantis, the eagle, the raven, the
sacred cow, some half-animal and half-human figures, the
goddess of mercy, the god of Canaan with thunderbolt and
lightning, and finally pictures of deified men such as Buddha
and Christ. We tried to find a degree of reasonableness in all
these symbols rather than to exalt one above the other; and
we closed with our own unanswered wonderings.

VI

What has been said regarding the questioning way of dealing
with theologies applies also to the way stories are told.

A good story is frequently the heart of a children's Meeting.
*In our telling of stories, we have cultivated the art of leaving
the children with questions to think about, rather than with
moral principles to apply.* We regard stories as opportunities
to enlarge children's experiences vicariously. Through the
story the child lives imaginatively for awhile in someone else's
shoes. As in real life, we would leave him free to draw his
own conclusions.

Indeed the spirit of inquiry may influence even the wording
of the initial words of the leader at the opening of the service.
The unifying thought or purpose of the gathering may be put
in the form of a question or of a wondering thought rather
than in the form of a pronouncement regarding God and his
holy dwelling place. Instead of presenting some affirmation
of belief on which to ask for meditation, such as the love of
God, or instead of taking some virtue, such as loyalty or courage or friendship, to illustrate and expand, it is more in
harmony with the natural approach to put the unifying thought
in the form of a problem to solve, a question to answer, or
some episode provocative of wonder, or an emotional problem
to which there is no answer.

A series of Meetings on the question, Should one always tell the truth? we found to be more thought-provoking than a series on honesty. Or a series on the question, What should one do when treated unfairly? was more interesting than a series on the need of self-control. The questions raised by the children themselves have proven to be among the very best themes for the general Meetings.

VII

We need also to do more basic thinking on how we pray in our services of worship. Too often our prayers are pe-titionary and expressions of praise for special blessings. We ask God to help us, to give us strength when we know that we have far more power already available to us than we are using. We ask God to bring peace when we know that we are the ones who have brought on our wars, and must be the ones to bring peace. We ask God to grant us his special blessings, to protect us from harm and tragedy, when we know that we can expect no special favors in such a universe as ours. We ask God to forgive us, when we ourselves harbor distrust and hate toward those who need our forgiveness. We ask God to search us and know our hearts, to try us and know our thoughts, and to see if there be any wicked way in us, when we know that it is we ourselves who must do the search-ing.

Prayer affords no magic way by which we may secure any of these blessings, yet we need to learn ways of increasing our awareness of the resources already ours. And we need from time to time words to express our deeper longings and concerns. Is not the evidence overwhelming that assures us that even the atom is linked to the universal, abiding vitality that binds all things in one? If we cannot separate the atom from God, how can we separate ourselves? Can we not still say with St. Paul that "neither death, nor life, nor angels, nor principalities, nor powers, nor things present, nor things to come, nor height, nor depth, nor any other creature, shall be able to separate us from" this universal life?[3] We have security surpassing the old Story of Salvation. None is excluded.

Perhaps it seems sentimental idealism to call this universal tie that seems to bind us in one cosmic union by the word *love*. Such love can scarcely be a simple duplicate on a larger scale of the love we know in our intimate personal relations. If "God is love," that love must be "broader than the measure of man's mind." As individuals we confess to feelings of little-ness in such a universal family that has in it both friend and foe, both man and beast, both material and spiritual things. Nevertheless is it not within this cosmic union that we must find our security and values? *To meditate and to wonder on some part of this universally felt Mystery is one way to wor-ship.* In it is the heart of that exercise of the spirit which gen-erations before us have long called by the name of worship.

When are children old enough to join us in such wondering and thoughtful meditation? We have learned through our contacts with children that on different age levels they have such moments of wistful wondering. We are often unable to detect the child's feeling tone. In the intimacies of the small family circle it may be easier to catch these emotional out-reachings than when we are together in the larger and more formal groups that meet in our churches. A leader's con-tinuing desire is to find out how to bring back into the chil-dren's memories such experiences as they may already have had secretly, but which they may have never been able to put into words. These are the experiences felt in some fleeting moment and then forgotten. Perhaps, as young Hilda Conklin once wrote, they "cannot always remember how it goes."

Our words of prayer with children may perhaps be ways of gathering up a few such wonderings. Such prayers, however, are seldom found in prayer books or in orders of service; and even if they are found, the reading of them from a book may bring only the sound of words like the tinkling of a cymbal.

In our experience with children we have found that our prayers need to be alive with the warmth of our own feelings. We believe that children need experiences deeply similar to what men have called prayer, but the feelings that come to them have a distinctly new flavor and require new words to bring them into bloom.

VIII

With our changing beliefs, perhaps the *very words "service of worship" need changing*. Think, for example, of the old culture that these words suggest. What is a "service"? What does it imply? That we gather to render a "service" demanded of us by God, our Almighty King. By so doing we gather merit for ourselves in his eyes. And what is worshiping? It is coming before God with our offerings, to praise his *worthship,* to proclaim his power and his majesty. When we stop to think about these antique symbols of God they seem strangely out of place in our society where kings are slowly traveling the road to oblivion. Most of us no longer come to church with the thought of doing a service for God, but to find help for ourselves. We come because we feel a need for the inspiration of the fellowship. We come because we want to share in a communal experience with our neighbors and friends. We come because we hope for a renewal of our strength, for some new insight, for better self-understanding. We want to be reminded of our religious heritage of nobility and courage. We want the windows of our spirits opened so that we may see to far horizons. We come for our own sakes, not to add honor to God's name.

The simple term "Meeting" used by the Friends seems more satisfying than "service of worship." We meet one another as companions in life's journey. We meet ourselves, and we become more aware of meeting God. As a result of such meetings we become conscious of our larger and deeper relationships. We are uplifted. A fresh purpose is lighted. Perhaps if we used this simpler term *Meeting* some of us might be released from our bondage to old patterns and "orders of service" so that we could experiment and search for ways that would better fulfill our modern needs.

More than a change of name is needed, however. Our dilemma is deep-rooted. The "Everlasting Arms" have become for us so large and vague that we cannot describe them. Indeed, some can no longer feel their warmth. The love of God has had to be so widened in order to be all-inclusive that we are prone to feel ourselves lost as individuals among multitudes. Perhaps our feelings of intimacy are fading. We believe, however, that our emerging faith can become tremendously powerful, and also intimately warm. It takes time, however, for new beliefs to take deep root in our cultural life. We are all together beginners reaching after clarity of thinking, wholeness of feeling and skills in leadership. We are standing on a threshold leading into an unknown but alluring territory.

IX

Children's Meetings need to be linked with other experiences. They need the enrichment of other group activities, just as much as the classroom work needs the general Meeting. To contemplate turning the church school into a children's church where only these services of worship are given importance is to defeat the very ends sought. The classroom activities should continually contribute to the content of the services of worship, and the services of worship should enrich the values gained in the smaller groups. Consequently, if the Meetings are to be vitally related to the children's real experiences, they must be guided by adults who keep in close touch with what is happening in the classes Sunday by Sunday. There must be a continuing interchange of experiences.

As the weeks pass, the leader will be on constant watch for suggestions for the Meetings coming from the children's activities in classes. He will encourage them to take complete charge of some Meetings when they wish to give a play that says something they want to say, or they have some subject they want thought about. The leader will gather from the teachers' weekly records, and from personal interviews with them, the questions the children are asking. Perhaps one of these questions may well be shared with the entire group at a Meeting.

X

If then we adhere to the general idea that services of worship need to be closely linked with the ongoing experiences of the various groups gathered in them, then it becomes essential that the *age range included in any one Meeting should not be so large and varied that such an exchange is unprofitable.* Our services of worship should be graded to children's understandings and experiences just as truly as our class work is. We defeat the purposes we cherish if we gather into these assemblies children either too old or too young to appreciate their meaning.

It is not necessary to have a large group together for a good Meeting. In fact small groups are an advantage, especially with the younger children. If room space is limited, these graded meetings need not be held all at the same hour. In one school the same room is used regularly for three different services of worship each Sunday morning.

In planning for the youngest children and for those of the early school ages, the most courageous and perhaps the most difficult changes in tradition are required. A basic question is this: When are children old enough to participate thoughtfully in a larger assembly than the single class affords? Should not the beginnings for the young children be found in informal quiet times, or in times for listening to a story or a poem, or in times for thinking together? If in the classroom work it is a reasoned policy to refrain from speaking of God because of the children's lack of maturity and readiness for the word, the achieving of the values sought by such a policy may be thwarted if these young children attend a service of worship, where prayers to God are spoken.

XI

We have found the need to experiment with different ways of keeping alive in children some awareness of the wonder that is in what is immediately theirs to touch and see and feel. We ourselves have had to learn to be more imaginative. We have had to practice the art of being curious about common and small things. We have had to remind ourselves over and over that there is an infinitely long story in every single thing in the universe — that we can pick up anything or stop to meditate on anything, and if we are persistent enough we may touch infinity. As Blake put it this infinity is even in a grain of sand. Sometimes children themselves are our teachers. Dorothy, aged eight, had been basking in the sun on a pile of sand, playing with her Irish setter, when she came into the house to find her mother. Carrying in her hand one single grain which she had picked up out of the big drab pile of sand, she wanted her mother to join her in wondering over its beautiful form and how it had come to be! Perhaps we need to become as children in order to recapture such a sensitive awareness of the intangible in little things.

We have therefore experimented with the practice of bringing simple things into the children's Meetings for contemplation: a bouquet of flowers, an egg, an orange, a stone, a few peanuts, or some fascinating piece of handicraft or work of art. Some simple question would initiate our meditation. "Suppose this flower could talk, what would we like to know? What would we want it to tell us?" Carl Sandburg has a wonderful poem on the egg. If the egg could answer him, he believes he would know everything.[4] Children like this kind of approach for it begins with something concrete that has reality for them.

We have experimented with other kinds of questions, dealing with immediate and present things. Children sometimes need to be surprised into awareness. Most living is superficial and even children become blasé toward the wonderful nature of existence. With some reticence, we report some examples of our efforts. The following are a few of the questions we have used.

1. "Suppose I owned everything in this room and promised I would give you anything in it you chose, provided you do not take with you anything that you cannot see or touch or weigh on some scales. What would you take?"

Interest in responding to this proposal usually increases as the children venture their suggestions and the leader challenges them. Slowly they come consciously into the presence of the "invisible ingredient" — the artist's thoughts and feelings, the craftsman's integrity, the laborer's patience and skill, the efforts of men in store and on farm, on freight trains and on trucks, as well as the age-long silent working of Mother Nature in soil and sunlight. All these and more are somehow to be found in the furniture of one room. Children at first may not go far in their pursuit of understanding, but they gain insight with each new and imaginative experience. In one class of nine-year-olds where this proposal was first discussed, one boy finally burst out with the remark, "Why you couldn't take a single thing in the whole world, because there is God." The vehemence with which he spoke, and the look in his eyes told the teacher that this boy had really discovered for himself a glimpse of God — "the intangible fact at the base of finite existence."

2. "What is the oldest thing in this room?" As the children respond to this question and consider one thing after another and tell what they know of its history, their amazement grows. Everything is old. It has always been difficult, even impossible, to say which is the oldest thing in the room. In one

group where this was talked over, the water in a glass on the table was singled out as old and its antiquity was traced back to the creation of the earth. In surprise Ruth said, "I looked at that glass of water, but it seemed so clean and fresh, I thought, 'It can't be old!' " With an imagination fresh as the water itself, Ruth put into words the wonder of our old earth, ever so new and young, and yet so old and enduring.

3. Another seemingly simple question brought forth one of the most moving experiences we ever participated in with children in a service of worship. The question this time was, "How old are you?" At first very definite answers were given by a number of children. They were nine, ten, and eleven. They had "begun" on their birthdays.

"But did they really begin the day they were born?" No, they began nine months before when the sperm entered the mother's womb.

"When did that sperm begin, or that other part in the mother that joined the sperm to make you, the egg that has grown into you?" That thought led us back to the grandparents. Once on the highroad to the past, the children's thinking traveled fast. Presently one boy said: "We will have to go all the way back to Adam and Eve."

"Yes, we have to go all the way back to the very first man and woman," said the leader. "You and I — every one of us then — is very old. Some part of us has been living all these thousands and thousands of years."

But even then we had not found when we began. We had to keep on going back and back to the very first living creatures, the one-celled individuals in the universal sea. We found our journey was endless. Finally the difference between sixty years and ten years of age seemed very small when compared to these millions of years. In fact the children were really as old as the leader herself: we were all old together![5]

The wonder of these ages of time really fired some of

the children with a great sense of worth, for they hurried back to their classroom where they could be alone with their teacher, and they cried out to her: "Hurray! Hurray! We are as old as you are! We are as old as you!" Such a glow of union with the ages is in truth a deeply religious experience.

XII

In this brief chapter on children's Meetings, we have attempted merely to suggest some of the most marked differences from the usual ways of worshiping that have been brought about because of our changed religious beliefs and because of our desire to experiment with a natural way of religious guidance. These brief jottings concerning children's Meetings — largely from personal experience — leave much unsaid. Only a few of the different types of gatherings for worship or group meditation have even been mentioned. The special problems arising when leading Meetings with children of different age-groups have been given little attention. These omissions are due partly to the desire not to lengthen a book which is already long. They are due also to the fact that there is so much still to learn. Very little serious experimentation has been carried on. Tradition still binds our churches to accepted patterns. New religious thinking is still being discouraged; and children's workers have been denied a fair opportunity for an adequate education. It is difficult to understand how the ministry to adults can require any more exacting skills or competence or religious insights than those that are needed by ministers to children.

If our religious beliefs have been changing and if they are to continue to change, our Meetings or services of worship must also change. We can no longer let prayer books, orders of service, printed readings and litanies do our thinking for us. Formality cannot be substituted for thoughtfulness or for sincerity in speech and song. Nor can the pageantry of robed

choirs and processionals and the grandeur of great music take
the place of the genuine emotional fires stirred by honest
intellectual searching.

It will take time for us who are adults to find as much
warmth of feeling in our relatedness within a universal cosmic
God as perhaps we once felt in our relations to a personal and
more limited God. Because of generations of ancestors nurtured in feelings of littleness and unworthiness and fear, it is
almost instinctive for us to be afraid of majesty and power.
Instead of standing up and looking into the face of the God
of this natural cosmos, we are prone like Moses to turn our
backs, feeling it is not safe to see.

But why should we think of a cosmic God only with fear
and trembling? Why fear the universal creative Life in whose
being we belong? Does the hand fear the mind that bids it
move? Does the heart fear the blood that surges through it?
Are we afraid of ourselves? If not, why fear the Greater Self
"in whom we live and move and have our being"? And why
think of a cosmic God as far off and cold — undiscoverable,
unapproachable? A cosmic God — if there be one — must
be closer than hands and feet. Nearer than a mother to her
unborn child. Our own relationships are boundless. They
are cosmic like those of God himself. We, too, are invisible,
intangible, and beyond understanding. We have the life blood
of God to warm and enliven our hearts. Why should we
wish for more?

Our new cosmologies, our new moralities, our new hope of
world brotherhood — when once they take deep root and
spread in our common social consciousness — will give us new
songs to sing, new experiences to celebrate, new depths of feeling to explore and new devotions to fire our zeal. Programs of
religious education should never cease to contribute a depth
and a height of feeling to children's living which public general
education does not commonly give. We need to use all the

ways possible and all the arts we know in helping children to keep their cups of experience full of health-giving emotions.

The depths of human experience are emotional, and vital religion will always fathom those depths. Nor is it the adult alone who has such possible depths. Children also feel deeply. But "each must plumb vastness and infinity. Let him call it what he will — fire, water, death, God, worlds, stars."[6] This the child must do *for* himself, but he cannot do it always *by* himself. He needs the feeling of honest and intimate togetherness with a group of his own kind. To encourage such a fellowship is goal enough for any leader in church or synagogue or family.

References

Chapter 1

IT MATTERS WHAT WE BELIEVE

Opening quotation: Einstein, Albert, *Out of My Later Years* (New York: Philosophical Library, 1950), p. 26. Quoted by permission of The Philosophical Library.

1. Jung, C. G., *Modern Man in Search of a Soul* (New York: Harcourt, Brace, 1933), p. 264. Quoted by permission of Harcourt, Brace and Company.
2. Macmurray, John, *Idealism Against Religion* (London: Lindsey Press, 1944). Pamphlet. Quoted by permission of The Lindsey Press.
3. Quoted by T. Morris Longstreth, "The Man Who Sought Peace with Himself," *The New York Times Magazine,* July 1, 1945.
4. Perry, Ruth Davis, *Children Need Adults* (New York: Harper, 1943). Quoted by permission of the author.

Chapter 2

IT MATTERS HOW WE GAIN OUR BELIEFS

Opening quotation: Lactantius, Lucius Firmianus, *The Divine Institutes* (written in the fourth century A.D.). In *Ante-Nicene Fathers,* Vol. VII (New York: Scribner's), 1899.

1. Frenkel-Brunswick, Else; Adorno, T. W.; Levinson, D. J.; and Sanford, R. N., *The Authoritarian Personality* (New York: Harper, 1949). Frenkel-Brunswick, Else, "A Study of Prejudice in Children," *Human Relations,* Vol. I (1948), No. 3. Material used by permission of Dr. Frenkel-Brunswick.
2. From a personal unpublished report by Mrs. Alice Owsley.

Chapter 3

NATURAL BEGINNINGS IN EARLY CHILDHOOD

Opening quotation: Sandburg, Carl, *The People, Yes* (New York, Harcourt, Brace, 1936), p. 208. Quoted by permission of Harcourt, Brace and Company.

1. Spitz, Rene, "Emotional Growth in the First Year," *Child Study,* Spring 1947.

2. Ribble, Margaret A., *The Rights of Infants, Early Psychological Needs and Their Satisfaction* (New York: Columbia University Press, 1947).
3. Erikson, Erik H., *A Healthy Personality for Every Child: A Digest of the Fact Finding Report of the Midcentury White House Conference on Children and Youth* (Raleigh, North Carolina: Health Publications Institute, 1950). Quoted by permission of the Children's Bureau, Federal Security Agency.
4. Ashley Montagu, M. F., *On Being Human* (New York: Henry Schuman, 1950), p. 92.
5. Aldrich, Charles A., and Aldrich, Mary M., *Babies are Human Beings* (New York: Macmillan, 1937), pp. 113, 114. Quoted by permission of The Macmillan Company.
6. Erikson, *A Healthy Personality*.
7. Timmins, Lois Fahs, in Chapter 1 of *Consider the Children: How They Grow,* by Elizabeth M. Manwell and Sophia L. Fahs, revised edition (Boston: Beacon Press, 1951), p. 10.
8. *Ibid,* p. 8.

Chapter 4
NATURAL BEGINNINGS IN CHILDHOOD'S CURIOSITIES

Opening quotation: Dixon, C. Madeleine, *High, Wide and Deep* (New York: John Day, 1938), pp. 128, 129. Quoted by permission of The John Day Company.

1. Wolff, Werner, *The Personality of the Preschool Child: His Search for His Self* (New York: Grune and Stratton, 1946), p. 14. Quoted by permission of Grune and Stratton, Inc.
2. *Ibid.,* p. 74.
3. Gesell, Arnold, and Ilg, Frances, *The Child From Five to Ten* (New York: Harper, 1940), p. 26.
4. Marrett, R. R., *Faith, Hope and Charity in Primitive Religion* (New York: Macmillan, 1932), p. 20.
5. The books referred to are the three volumes of the "Martin and Judy" series, by Verna Hills and Sophia L. Fahs (Boston: Beacon Press, 1939-1943).
6. See the introductions to Volumes I and II of the "Martin and Judy" series.
7. Manwell, Elizabeth M., and Fahs, Sophia L., *Consider the Children: How They Grow,* revised edition (Boston: Beacon Press, 1951).

Chapter 5
THE OLD BIBLE: THE STORY OF SALVATION

Opening quotation: Burroughs, John, *Accepting the Universe* (Boston: Houghton Mifflin, 1920), pp. 117, 118. Quoted by permission of Houghton Mifflin Company.

1. Jarrell, Hampton M., "Sunday Schools Don't Teach," *The Atlantic Monthly,* December 1950. Quoted by permission of *The Atlantic Monthly.*
2. Augustine, in *The Nicene and Post Nicene Fathers of the Christian Church,* edited by Philip Schaff (New York: Christian Literature Society, 1887), First Series, Vol. III, pp. 302-310.
3. Mark 16: 15; Matthew 28: 20.
4. Revelation 21: 4.
5. Revelation 21: 27.
6. Revelation 19: 1, 2a.
7. Revelation 19: 6-7.
8. Revelation 20: 10, 15.
9. Revelation 22: 19.

Chapter 6
THE BIBLE — NEWLY INTERPRETED

Opening quotation: Whitman, Walt, "Carol of Occupations," in *Leaves of Grass* (New York: Doubleday, 1924). Quoted by permission of Doubleday and Company.

1. Arnold, W. H., *Ephod and Ark: A Study of the Records and Religion of the Ancient Hebrews* (Cambridge: Harvard University Press, 1917).
2. Exodus 19: 5.
3. Breasted, James H., *The Dawn of Conscience* (New York: Scribner's, 1933), pp. 15, 38. Quoted by permission of Charles Scribner's Sons.
4. Albright, W. F., *Archaeology and the Religion of Israel* (Baltimore: Johns Hopkins Press, 1942).
5. Flight, John W., *The Drama of Ancient Israel* (Boston: Beacon Press, 1949).
6. Waterman, Leroy, "Biblical Studies in a New Setting," *Journal of Biblical Literature,* Vol. LXVI (1947). Quoted by permission of the author.

Chapter 7
THE NEED FOR BOTH BIBLES — AND MORE

1. Ross, Floyd H., *Addressed to Christians* (New York: Harper, 1950), p. 45. Quoted by permission of the author.
2. MacLean, Angus H., *Planning the Religious Education Curriculum* (Boston: Beacon Press, 1951). Pamphlet.

Chapter 8
OLD AND NEW COSMOLOGIES

Opening quotation: Whitman, *op. cit.* Quoted by permission of Doubleday and Company.

1. Bok, J. Bart, "The Milky Way," *Scientific American,* February 1950.
2. Hubble, Edwin P., "Five Historic Photographs from Palomar," *Scientific American,* November 1949.
3. Bok, *op. cit.*
4. Dobzhansky, Theodosius, "The Genetic Basis of Evolution," *Scientific American,* January 1950.
5. Hurley, P. M., "Radioactivity and Time," *Scientific American,* August 1949.
6. Hoyle, Fred, *The Nature of the Universe* (New York: Harper, 1951), p. 123. Quoted by permission of Harper and Brothers.
7. Cuenot, L. C., *Invention et finalité en biologie* (Paris: Flammarion, 1941).
8. Dobzhansky, *op. cit.*
9. Mayer, Charles, *Man: Mind or Matter,* translated and with a preface by Harold Larrabee (Boston: Beacon Press, 1951), p. 16.
10. Dobzhansky, *op. cit.* Quoted by permission of *Scientific American.*
11. From a personal report to the author by the mother, Mrs. Alice Owsley.
12. Whitehead, Alfred North, *Essays in Science and Philosophy* (New York: Philosophical Library, 1947), p. 90. Quoted by permission of The Philosophical Library.
13. Reiser, Oliver L., *Scientific Humanism as Creative Morality* (Girard, Kansas: Haldeman-Julius, 1949).
14. Mayer, *op. cit.,* p. 29.
15. Steinbach, H. B., "Animal Electricity," *Scientific American,* February 1950.
16. Genesis 1: 28.
17. Shelley, Percy Bysshe, from a poem "Love's Philosophy."
18. Frank, Lawrence K., *Nature and Human Nature* (New Brunswick, New Jersey: Rutgers University Press, 1951), pp. 38, 39. Quoted by permission of Dr. Lawrence K. Frank and Rutgers University Press.
19. Macmurray, John, *Reason and Emotion* (New York: Appleton-Century, 1938), p. 65. Quoted by permission of Appleton-Century-Crofts.
20. Mayer, *op. cit.*
21. Peattie, Donald Culross, "The Eternal Story," *Country Gentleman,* January 1941.
22. Ashley Montagu, M. F., "Social Instincts," *Scientific American,* April 1950. Quoted by permission of *Scientific American.*
23. John 12: 24.
24. I Corinthians 15: 17.

Chapter 9
OLD AND NEW MORALITIES

Opening quotation: Bynner, Witter, *The New World* (New York: Mitchell Kennerley, 1916), p. 38. Quoted by permission of the author.

1. Baruch, Dorothy W., *Glass House of Prejudice* (New York: Morrow, 1946), pp. 93-95. Quoted by permission of the author.
2. Allen, Frederick H., *Psychotherapy with Children* (New York: Norton, 1942), p. 260.
3. Chisholm, C. Brock, *The Psychiatry of Enduring Peace and Social Progress* (William Allanson White Psychiatric Foundation: Offprinted from *Psychiatry*, February 1946).
4. Mark 2: 14-17.

Chapter 10
AN OLD AND A NEW WORLD BROTHERHOOD

Opening quotation: Martin, Alfred W., from an unpublished address.

1. Luke 6: 27.
2. Horney, Karen, *Our Inner Conflicts: A Constructive Theory of Neurosis* (New York: Norton, 1945).
3. Macmurray, *Idealism Against Religion.* Quoted by permission of The Lindsey Press.
4. Schoen, Max, *The Man Jesus Was* (New York: Knopf, 1950), p. 214. Quoted by permission of Dr. Max Schoen and Alfred A. Knopf, Inc.
5. *Li Chi or Book of Rites,* unpublished translation by Dr. D. Willard Lyon, VII: 2.

Chapter 11
THE ART OF GROUP LEADERSHIP

Opening quotation: From *Platform-Recommendations and Pledge to Children of the Midcentury White House Conference on Children and Youth,* 1950 (Raleigh, North Carolina: Health Publications Institute, 1950). Quoted by permission of the Children's Bureau, Federal Security Agency.

1. From a personal report to the author by Ruth D. Perry, director of the nursery and kindergarten of the Riverside Church, New York City.
2. From a personal report to the author by Mrs. Edith Dewey, when directing the work in the Unitarian Church, Wilmington, Delaware.
3. Fahs, Sophia L., *Beginnings of Earth and Sky* (Boston: Beacon Press, 1937).

4. This account is taken mainly from the records of Alice Cobb, teacher of the fourth grade of the junior department of the church school of Riverside Church, New York City.
5. Personal letter, quoted by permission of Dr. Albert Einstein.
6. This account is taken mainly from the records of Emily Ellis, teacher of the sixth grade of the church school of Riverside Church, New York City.

Chapter 12
WHAT SHALL CHILDREN STUDY?

Opening quotation: Manwell and Fahs, *op. cit.*

1. Whitman, Walt, "There Was a Child Went Forth," in *Leaves of Grass.*
2. Manwell, Elizabeth M. and Fahs, Sophia L., *Growing Bigger* (Boston: Beacon Press, 1942).
3. Adler, Alfred, *Social Interest: A Challenge to Mankind* (New York: Putnam's, 1938), pp. 282, 283. Quoted by permission of G. P. Putnam's Sons.
4. Jacks, L. P., *My Neighbor the Universe* (New York: Putnam's, 1929), p. 80. Quoted by permission of G. P. Putnam's Sons.
5. *Ibid.,* p. 52.
6. Fahs, Sophia L., *From Long Ago and Many Lands* (Boston: Beacon Press, 1948).
7. Fahs, Sophia L. and Spoerl, Dorothy T., *Beginnings of Life and Death* (Boston: Beacon Press, 1938).
8. Edwards, Margaret D., *Child of the Sun* (Boston: Beacon Press, 1939).

Chapter 13
HOW ABOUT WORSHIPING TOGETHER?

Opening quotation: Fahs, Sophia L., "The Beginnings of Mysticism in Children's Growth," *Religious Education,* May-June 1950.

1. MacLean, *op. cit.*
2. Recent song books for children include *Martin and Judy Songs,* compiled by Edith Lovell Thomas (Boston: Beacon Press, 1948); and *The Whole World Singing,* compiled by Edith Lovell Thomas (New York: Friendship Press, 1950).
3. Romans 8: 38, 39.
4. Sandburg, Carl, *Good Morning, America!* (New York: Harcourt, Brace, 1928).
5. See also the chapter "Our Own Wonderings About Death" in Fahs and Spoerl, *op. cit.*
6. Dixon, *op. cit.*